MY SIDE OF THE RIVER

MY SIDE OF THE RIVER

A Memoir

Elizabeth Camarillo Gutierrez

ST. MARTIN'S PRESS
NEW YORK

First published in the United States by St. Martin's Press, an imprint of St. Martin's Publishing Group

MY SIDE OF THE RIVER. Copyright © 2024 by Elizabeth Camarillo Gutierrez. All rights reserved. Printed in the United States of America. For information, address St. Martin's Publishing Group, 120 Broadway, New York, NY 10271.

www.stmartins.com

Designed by Gabriel Guma

The Library of Congress Cataloging-in-Publication Data is available upon request.

ISBN 978-1-250-27795-4 (hardcover)
ISBN 978-1-250-27796-1 (ebook)

Our books may be purchased in bulk for promotional, educational, or business use. Please contact your local bookseller or the Macmillan Corporate and Premium Sales Department at 1-800-221-7945, extension 5442, or by email at MacmillanSpecialMarkets@macmillan.com.

First Edition: 2024

10 9 8 7 6 5 4 3 2 1

To Fer and to all the younger siblings like him:
remember to do the dishes.

CONTENTS

MY SIDE OF THE RIVER

Prologue

_____

THE RIVER

Signs along the road, which was cracked and littered with pot-holes from previous rains, told us and anyone who cared to look that we were close to the Rillito River. The signs served to warn people of the unpredictable nature of flash floods, hoping to deter them from crossing through the river when it rained. I didn't need the signs to know that we were close; I could draw the path to the river in my head and in the dirt with a stick all the same. I had always been aware of the river's presence, had known my way there and my way back home since we'd first arrived in Tucson when I was four.

My mom and dad simply called the river El Rillito. That is, unless they were mad or short on time. Then the river became an obstacle, and its name simply became El Río. It was a funny way to punish its existence. By taking away the *ito* by which any word in Spanish can be made cute or lovable or little, they tried to diminish its beauty.

Of course, the rivers in Southern Arizona aren't really rivers. They're dry and arid and for the most part completely unremarkable. The Rillito River seemed particularly useless apart from the fact that it divides the city of Tucson nearly in half, politely segregating the immigrant households south of it from the pristine white manicured homes to the north. Even still, nobody paid much attention to the Rillito until the summer of 2006, when a monsoon filled up the dry riverbed for the first time in years, transforming the dusty canal into a roaring monster. That summer, my parents made a big deal out of it, herding me and my four-year-old brother, Fernando, into the car after the rain stopped to drive us over to the river's edge.

When we arrived, I stared, transfixed by the powerful sound of moving water. I'd learned at school that the river was full of invasive species threatening the delicate balance of the desert. I took this opportunity to see if there was anything else that stood out. Out of the corner of my eye, I followed a spare car part as it floated from east to west, disappearing under dark muddy water. Somewhere beneath the surface, the river took bits and pieces of the city, violently dismantling things that were once whole. I wondered how the desert, a place with such a rough exterior, always seemed so vulnerable and at risk. The only other things I could see were the tips of half-submerged carrizo, a river reed I always confused with bamboo. I sighed, unsure if the carrizo was native to the riverbed, remembering the way my abuelo Marcelino had taught me how to use it to make kites back in Mexico. Regardless of the carrizo's official status, it lived here in the Rillito.

On the drive back home, I asked my parents if the river had ever been a *normal* river, one that ran year-round, that wasn't dry; one that did what a river was supposed to do. Perhaps my mom answered first, or it might have been my dad. What I do remember is that I was presented with a list of incomplete yet reasonable explanations. "Pues claro, of course the river used to run," Mom murmured.

"Sí, antes sí, mijita, hace mucho tiempo," Dad continued. I watched as he furrowed his black eyebrows, glancing back at me through the rearview mirror. "A long time ago, the river used to run, but now it doesn't."

"Why not?" I asked.

"Global warming, dams—por muchas razones," he continued. "Ese agua, it used to even make its way all the way down to Mexico. Not anymore."

Over the years, I watched the local news capitalize on the occasional flooding of the river brought on by the monsoons. They sold us the cliché miracle of rain in the desert through videos of shirtless men on canoes rowing through flooded streets before eventually getting back to what they normally liked to show: petty theft, dangerous immigrants, and property damage. After the first days of rainfall, the charm wore off and everyone began to demonize the river instead. Nobody wanted to remember the state that the river was in before or the state that the river would return to. Nobody cared to think about why the river was usually dry and why the indigenous plants that once flourished kept dying. Instead, people complained about being late as roads closed due to flooding. When the river decided to *act* like a river, it was no longer endearing.

In many ways the river taught me about life: that wealth and poverty are in proximity, but always separated; that people don't like what they can't control, preferring instead to reward you only when you fulfill their narrative about who you are supposed to be; that there are seasons of lack and plenty, of drought and flooding. In many ways, my life would mirror the river and its seasons, full of living things fighting to survive among invasive species. But in one way my life would never mirror the river: I would always return to Mexico.

PART ONE

1

BE THE BEST

In the weeks before we moved to the United States, I watched my parents pack boxes of things in our Costa Rican home—where we briefly lived for a job my dad temporarily had—that we'd eventually leave behind: my dollhouse, a small pink chair, my favorite toys. "We'll start fresh," Mom would promise. "There's so much more to look forward to." I was a toddler, too young to understand the permanence of goodbyes or the uncertainty of the adventures I was assured I would experience. Instead, I grew excited, and when planes flew above us, I'd point my finger into the sky at the vapor trails streaming behind them.

"I'm going to fly to America," I'd say.

Most people think that immigrants move from one country to another, establish a new life, and never look back. My parents didn't do that—they were nomads, a characteristic of people who live close to the border. Growing up in Mexico, my parents knew they could always hop over to the United States on tourist visas to go to the malls or Costco. But when the economy got bad, tourist visas became an opportunity for people like my parents. An opportunity to get eyes on signs reading HELP WANTED or EN BUSCA DE LAVAPLATOS plastered in front of busy American restaurants. Restaurants that didn't care about tourist visas, green cards, or any so-called necessary paperwork. They wanted Brown hands, and my dad happened to have two of them.

Before I was born, my mom and dad had visited America many times. Sometimes it was for a month as my dad bought and resold cars. Other times, he would get a more stable gig, like the time he became a celebrated chef in one of Arizona's steakhouse chains. "La carne nomás necesita un poco de sal," he'd say. "Meat needs nothing more than the right amount of salt." But everything was temporary. Jobs would end, needs would change, and my parents would pack up and leave again. Sometimes they went back to Mexico; other times, they'd find themselves jobs in Spanish-speaking places like Costa Rica. But when my mom got pregnant with me, she knew she'd have to go back to the United States. From the moment she wanted children, she wanted them to be American. No matter how hugely pregnant she grew, she was determined to waddle her ass over the border before I was born if that's what it took.

My mom stayed true to her promise, and a few months later, in the fall of 1995, I came into the world in a hospital in Tucson. My mom gushed at the sight of me at the hospital nursery, surrounded by a sea of crying white blobs. She didn't see an "anchor baby," she just saw *her* baby. A small Brown little raisin covered in a fine layer of dark hair. When the doctor handed me over to my mom, he chuckled at the fuzz. "She's like a monkey," he said. "Pendejo," Mom replied. "Es perfecta."

My dad wasn't around when I was born but rushed to Tucson from work as soon as he heard that my mom was in labor. When he finally held me, all he could say was, "Es un regalo perfecto." She's the perfect gift.

"She almost had the same birthday as you," my mom replied. "She just didn't want to wait." After spending weeks in Tucson waiting for my arrival, my mom was itching to go back to Mexico and ready the rest of the family to meet me. After I recovered from a severe case of jaundice, my dad packed us up and drove to Mexico. It would be four years before my parents moved us to American soil again—this time with plans to stay in Arizona for a while so that I'd one day be able to go to an American school. Sometime in 1999, I found myself in the back seat of a used car full of things my parents thought we'd need for our new life in the States.

While we waited in line to cross the border, my mom held our passports—my navy blue American passport was sandwiched between their green Mexican ones. It was a booklet that made me different and gave me things my parents couldn't have, even if I didn't realize it at the time. When the border patrol agent eventually asked for our papers, my mom handed the passports over, and the agent glanced at the picture next to my name. "Is your name Elizabeth?" he asked. "Yes, like the queen," I replied. With a chuckle, he let us all through.

For the next hour, I stared out of the window and took in the Arizona desert. The landscape was littered with hundred-year-old saguaros. Eventually we made it back to Tucson and drove into a quiet trailer park. My dad parked on the street outside of a pink sun-bleached motor home.

"Ya llegamos," my dad announced. My mom and I looked at each other, unimpressed but ready to stretch our legs. Slowly, I took in what would be my first home in America, one we would share with my tío Miguel and his own growing family of three. Adult me might have envisioned the energy of a city like New York or the glamour of Los Angeles when picturing my arrival to the United States, but that first night, we all slept on mattresses on the floor in one of the bedrooms while Tío Miguel and his family did the same in the other.

My dad had split the cost of the trailer with his brother, but it was solely in Uncle Miguel's name because he had a Social Security number and Dad didn't. He was a numbers guy, so he figured if he divided everything with Miguel for a while, both families would be better off. My mom, who didn't trust my uncle, was pissed.

"Nos vamos a quedar sin nada," she warned. "We're going to end up with nothing to our name." Still, she managed to keep me busy and unaware of the tension. Within the chaos, the lack of permanence and stability, Mom and I built forts out of crisp white sheets that smelled like Downy. As I poked my head up from underneath, I'd find myself staring at the way my mom looked. She was beautiful, her brown eyes framed by thick eyebrows, her features delicate and classic. I stared as the morning light would shine on her thick hair, making it look like the colors of a sunset in the summer. "Te encontré, I found you!" my mom would squeal, wrapping me up and lifting me up into the air.

Before long, my dad took his resourcefulness to Craigslist,

scouring other people's unwanted stuff to fix up our space while saving the money from the odd jobs he took. He recarpeted the rooms in a plain brown low-pile rug and furnished the living room with sturdy secondhand sofa beds, a vintage chest coffee table, and a TV cabinet made of what he called "good wood." When I complained about our small living space or having to share it with other family members, my dad would shake his head and pull at the hairs on his chin. Though he shaved every morning, his stubble always grew back in quickly. My dad was proper that way, well-kept, his black hair always gelled and combed in a side part. His eyes crinkling into a smile, he would exclaim, "Don't worry. This is just temporary."

Eventually my parents formed a steady routine, but the best parts of it were always the weekends. We'd all hop in the Jeep Cherokee my dad had fixed up and drive to yard sales in the gated neighborhoods across the river. We'd head up into the mountains, where gorgeous adobe brick houses with pools lined the dips and crevices of the horizon. Sometimes we saw people who looked like us, sweat soaking their shirts as they worked on the beautiful landscaping, keeping it perfectly manicured. Peering out of our rolled-down windows, we'd imagine a life we couldn't afford. After all, we were there to buy what the rich people discarded. We could always find furniture, knickknacks, and things we saw value in—items we could fix up or flip for more money. "When you're older, you should buy a home here," Dad would say, eyeing the architecture. "Even if it's a small bit of land, maybe half an acre, that's all you need." Unsure of what to do with his impromptu lessons on real estate, I'd nod and think to myself, *Isn't he the one supposed to be buying us a home?*

Occasionally we'd drive south instead of north, staying on our side of the river. If we drove long enough, we'd find ourselves in El Sur—a predominantly Mexican neighborhood that became an official city in 1940, forever separating it from the rest of Tucson. In many ways, driving through South Tucson felt like a drive through pueblos in Mexico. On the sidewalks, set up in the front yards of houses with bad paint jobs and rusted gates, were tacos and Sonoran hot dog stands. Little kids, dark and sunburnt, would ride their bikes in the middle of empty streets. Despite its liveliness, this neighborhood was known for its high crime rates and poor-performing schools. Whenever we'd visit the Mexican shops or the swap meet in El Sur, my dad locked up the steering wheel with a giant metal bar to deter thieves. "No podemos confiar," he'd grumble. "You can't be too careful."

My parents talked about South Tucson as if it were a dirty place, but that didn't stop me from liking it. When I was there, I felt fun and rebellious, and I liked that I blended in with crowds of Mexican kids at the park. There people didn't care about how loud they blasted their music as they drove lowriders with tire rims my dad called tacky. In South Tucson, Mexicans seemed to make the rules. People seemed happier there, more relaxed, but whenever I'd ask Dad if we could move to El Sur, he'd always tell me the same thing. "Para qué? Es muy feo ahí. What for? It's so ugly over there." My parents had a clear idea of what they wanted to represent. I never understood exactly what that was, but I knew what it *wasn't*: it was clear from the clothes we wore, the church we went to, and most important, the school their American daughter would go to that they didn't want to be perceived as poor, *uneducated* Mexican immigrants.

———————

Within weeks of our arrival in Tucson, I had a weekday routine, too. In the mornings, my mom would yell at me from the kitchen, "Elizabeth, ya despiértate, come have breakfast." If I didn't get up quickly enough, she'd stomp right up to me in bed, a spoon in hand. "Ándale, you're going to be late for school." By the time I got to the table, my plate of beans, eggs, and tortillas would be set next to my dad's. Sometimes, my tía Rocio would barge in, taking up space in the kitchen to make food for my twiggy little cousins. My mornings always smelled like coffee with a splash of chaos. Someone was always angry or late or in a rush, but somehow I was always on time for preschool.

If my parents could have enrolled me in preschool before they even got to the United States, they would have. They were obsessed with my education, neurotic even, but my insatiable desire to be told I was smart made it easier for them. I was known at preschool for carrying around a picture dictionary while asking the teachers, "How do you say ___?" Within six months, I had learned English, and my parents, *logically*, came to the conclusion that I was a gifted prodigy. From there, my parents began to methodically research different elementary schools in the area. They listened to gossip and spoke to the people at church about it. Dad had spent a few years at a fancy university in Mexico City before dropping out, and he knew the value of a proper education and the connections it could create. My mother, who was innately smart and inquisitive, had less schooling than my dad, having dropped out sometime in middle school and gone on to secretary school, which I still can't believe was actually a thing. She learned how to type and had a government job before marrying my dad. They both knew from experience that the world simply wouldn't favor a Brown uneducated Mexican girl. They knew how much of an advantage a good American education would be for their American daughter. They wanted the best for me.

———————

The school closest to our home was Laguna Elementary School, which my freckled, red-haired neighbor Kayla had briefed me about. "You and I can hang out during recess," she said. "I'm already popular, so you can meet everyone I know." What I didn't realize was that my parents never intended to send me there. The thing about Laguna was that people *like us* went to school there. That is to say, Brown kids who spoke broken English *and* broken Spanish. And as far as my parents were concerned, places that served Brown kids and immigrants were not good enough for their Brown daughter of immigrants. The facilities were old, the location was bad, and the teachers and students seemed to have a negative reputation. There was no fit big enough for me to throw that would make them change their minds. Resolutely, my parents said I would absolutely not be going there. "You'll just be another one, another poor Brown girl from the neighbor-hood," Mom announced, exasperated. "Sí, está lleno de nacos y cholos," Dad added. "Those kids will just end up in gangs."

My parents were prepared to drive me across town if it meant I could go to a good school. The nicest schools were close to the beautiful homes we'd see at the foot of the Catalina Moun-tains when we were going to yard sales. They were pristine and well-kept, overlooking the city with their impressive views of the valley. The neighborhoods themselves were composed of well-off families and snowbirds from places like Iowa and Canada—people who'd come down to Arizona for the endless warmth. Some of their homes weren't made of the typical adobe; some chose bright white colors for their homes, speckling the mountains. Their white walls and pristine green lawns seemed to sparkle among the mesquite trees and saguaros growing in the red and brown clay of the valley. The desert was always full of contrasts.

Day after day, my mom and dad would enter the clean, air-conditioned offices at the schools, where Dad would proudly and loudly speak in broken English about how qualified I was to attend. My parents received rejection after rejection, being told the school couldn't accept me because we lived in the wrong zip code, as if that excuse would make a difference to them. They might have fallen off their high horse and were quickly going through their savings by relocating to the United States, but they didn't come here to put me in a school worse than the ones in Mexico. They weren't about to sacrifice my future—*our* future—and their image because we lived on the wrong side of the river.

A few weeks later, we heard about Richardson Elementary School from one of the Mexican moms who had a kid at the preschool I went to. "Es una escuela muy buena, it's a really good school," she said to my mom, wagging her finger in the air. "If you need to, you can use our address to sign up," she continued in a whisper. "We live in the district. They have a great kindergarten program."

Mom smiled. "Gracias, we'll let you know," she said, narrowing her eyes as she made a mental note. Because Richardson was out of our zip code, putting a different address down would make it possible for me to enroll. While it wasn't necessarily the most scrupulous, my mom made moves. She would have been a shark had she had the education to become a lawyer or work on Wall Street. Sure, there was the risk of arrest or deportation, but Mom wasn't used to losing. At least not when it came to her little girl.

It turned out there was no need to lie about where we came from or where we lived. The staff at Richardson waved my well-dressed parents in, assuring them it would all be okay. "Doesn't matter if she's out of district, hun, just make sure she keeps up her grades," said the school secretary. "You can call me Mrs. Sabrina." She winked.

When I first walked into Richardson, things felt different. Richardson was clean and well-kept. Everywhere I looked there seemed to be order; things moved along like a well-oiled machine. On a plaque above the blue front doors stood a bold quote, which to this day is still seared in my brain: *Our Future Walks Through These Doors.* This was a place that seemed to care about what would become of me. "I'm the future," I repeated to myself.

Inside, the hallways were bright and lined with the pictures of those on the honor roll tacked on top of colorful kraft paper. The library was huge and run by a welcoming librarian with silvery white hair. She kept pets inside, including a black widow she housed in a jar and an iguana who sat on top of a bookshelf. She had somehow managed to hang a giant model airplane from the ceiling, which the fire department would later take down, claiming it was a hazard. The playground was large and tidy, with a giant hill covered in green grass, bright flowers, and annoying sticky seeds that got all over your clothes when you rolled down it.

By the time the first day of kindergarten rolled around, I was over the fact that I wouldn't get to go to school with my neighborhood friend Kayla. With my mom's hand gripping mine tightly, I was led to my classroom. Kids wearing new shoes and carrying new backpacks ran down the halls beside us. Confidently, my mother introduced herself to Ms. Brown. "Soy su mama," she said. "Cuídamela."

My new teacher nodded shyly before responding, "Muy poco español." Still, she seemed to get the gist of what Mom had said. Before I ran to my seat, I felt Mom squat next to me, her brown eyes leveling to mine. "Elizabeth, tú tienes que ser la mejor. You have to be the best." My small body was high on energy and nerves. "You don't have to tell anyone that you're the best, but you have to be." I stood there, looking back at her, confused by her proposal. I was to be great, but I was to do it modestly. "Está bien, Mama," I replied. "I'll be the best." I couldn't have imagined all the ways her belief would continually empower me, and all the ways the pressure of that belief would eventually debilitate me.

2

THE MOVIE THEATER

I grew up watching my mom be brave. She stood up to my dad and my uncles, never cowering in the way I'd seen other Mexican moms do. She held her ground, her calm and resolute attitude only making the men around her angrier. "Todos somos iguales," Mom said. "No authority or person has the right to belittle you."

Sometimes Dad chimed in. "Y menos porque tú eres ciudadana," he added with a smile. "Nobody can do anything to you." Before I even understood the concept of citizenship, I knew I was protected in a way that they weren't. They were always aware of authority figures, making themselves smaller around cops and the law, hiding—something I didn't feel the need to do. "If you ever feel unsafe, go to the police," my parents instructed. Unlike them, I didn't need to hide.

My mom also didn't like relying on my dad for money, and a few months after I started kindergarten, she'd gotten herself a job thanks to whisper networks. Mom had sourced information about where she could work the same way that most people without the right papers do: through the gossip and hearsay of those who came before them. For some, whisper networks led them to random corners in front of Home Depots. "Sí vas a las siete de la mañana, mi amigo tiene trabajo," someone would hear. The next day at 7 A.M.—not a minute later—people would show up ready to work. Nobody knew who the "amigo" picking them up would be. All they knew is they'd get paid in cash.

Whisper networks were meant to protect people, and that was especially the case in 2001. Two months after 9/11, people could feel the tension as anti-immigrant rhetoric spread across the news. My parents, who always had the radio tuned to the Spanish stations, would keep tabs on the announcements of raids from radio hosts, who described scenes of immigrants getting corralled like cattle and shuttled to places like Eloy, where there was a private detention camp profiting from each faceless Brown immigrant they could get their grimy hands on. We rarely saw ourselves reflected on the TV screen except for when we were treated like animals, lined up and put into vans. Whisper networks helped keep people hidden and safe.

My mom's connection to the whisper networks started with after-school small talk. Somehow she had become besties with every Spanish-speaking mom at Richardson, as she took me to picnics and birthday parties in the park. At some point Lucrecia, a classmate's mom, mentioned an opportunity. "You know, I heard they needed someone to clean the movie theater down at the Foothills Mall," she said. Before long, contact information was exchanged among swarms of screaming children. "Show up at the movie theater close to midnight," Lucrecia whispered, leaning into Mom with a big smile on her face.

I don't think my mom thought much about the raids or the risk of working in the United States without the right papers. She wanted a job—any job—that would let her have some semblance of economic freedom. She wanted the Alma bag from Louis Vuitton and leather loafers from Nordstrom. She was tired of spending time clipping coupons to lower grocery bills. She was tired of asking my dad for money and then having to explain herself. So promptly at midnight, my mom showed up to the theater along with a lady named Lupita. Mom figured that if she worked a night job, she could make money while making sure to still take care of food and her other responsibilities during the day. Dad was supportive because, after all, we needed the cash.

A man named Luís let my mom and Lupita in, shrugging his shoulders as he offered them the job. "You start now," he said, pointing toward a couple of carts filled with cleaning supplies and mops. "Good luck. Some movie called *Harry Potter* came out and the kids went crazy."

That night, Mom and Lupita hauled away mountains of popcorn and scraped sticky, syrupy spills from the floors of the slanted theaters. By the time the sun rose the next day, she realized the floor-to-ceiling windows by the entrance of the theater were still smudged with a thick layer of oily fingerprints and synthetic butter waiting to be wiped off. By that point, she didn't have any fucks left to give and she walked out, hoping nobody would notice or care. The first thing Mom said when she walked back home was "Who the *fuck* is Harry Potter?"

The next day Mom showed up to work late in the evening as the last showings of the films were winding up. Lupita was a no-show after realizing what being a janitor in a movie theater actually entailed, leaving Mom with twelve rooms to clean on her own. Luís also didn't care to help my mom—he handled his wing of the theater and left without a word. Panicked, Mom called my dad, who left me in my aunt and uncle's care and came equipped with a leaf blower to gather the popcorn into manageable piles.

Management gave no vacation days. You missed a day, you got fired. If it was an emergency, workers found replacements, hoping that management wouldn't be able to distinguish one Brown person from another. That Christmas, Luís went home to Mexico and never came back. He attempted to fill his spot with a replacement, Ana, who showed up for only half a night, half-assing her work and leaving a mess behind her. My mom, faced with cleaning the entirety of the theater, again called Dad for help. My parents fell into a peaceful rhythm as they cleaned the theater night after night because it was what had to be done. There was no other choice.

Often my parents took me to the movie theater with them. We'd go late at night when the stragglers or people who'd fallen asleep had already been ushered out and my parents could let themselves in with a special key given only to maintenance staff that provided access to everything except the concession stand cabinets. My mom, who was always cold, would wrap me delicately in thick blankets for the ten-minute car ride. I usually slept the whole way there and, still small enough to be carried, didn't really feel the handoff from my mom to my dad. I knew that if I pretended to be asleep, I could burrow my face into the protective warmth of Dad's prickly, half-shaved neck.

Once we were inside, Mom would take over one of the benches outside of the theater rooms. She'd spray it with a bottle of diluted bleach, wiping it dry before layering it with blankets and a pillow. Dad would heave me over his shoulder as gently as possible, tucking me in and hoping I'd be able to sleep through the night. They didn't want me to nod off while I was in school.

I started going to the movie theater with them because my tía Rocio was not okay. After we had lived a few months with her, my tío Miguel, and my cousins, it became clear as day that there was something going on below the surface. Sometimes my tía's issues were minor. She'd forget a thing or two. Other days she was fatigued, going about her days with catatonic carelessness. Cabinets were left open, dirty dishes remained unwashed. Other days she was active, speaking quickly, her sentences fragmented. My parents liked calling my tía "La Loca." At night, I'd listen to them laughing as I fell asleep.

"She forgot that she was carrying Andre," Mom said. "When she opened the freezer, she smacked him with the door."

"You can't make this shit up," Dad replied. Eventually, though, things became serious. My aunt's forgetfulness spread to things that one simply *can't* forget, like a pot on the stove or picking her kids up from school. Time and time again my parents would receive calls from the school's front desk. "Hi, your niece and nephew are still waiting for their parents to pick them up. Can you come and get them?"

At first, Mom tried to reason with my aunt. They shared a kitchen, bathroom, and roof—like it or not, my mom had to figure out how to live with her. After many failed attempts, my mom realized it was pointless. When my aunt's kids needed her, she was asleep in her room with the door locked. When she cooked fish—which was all the time—she'd leave the stinky dishes in the sink for days, grinding my mom's gears until she angrily scrubbed them herself. Mom wasn't quiet about her frustration, though; she let me and my cousins and even the neighbors know when she was mad. You could hear everything through the trailer's walls.

"Pinche loca, you left the stove on!" Mom screamed. Sometimes, she tried to follow my aunt to her room, attempting to get a word in. Instead of having a conversation, my aunt covered her ears and yelled, "Ya déjame en paz!" I observed these fights often from the kitchen table or while watching television, but sometimes I turned the TV off. There was no telenovela chaotic enough to compete with my mom chasing my aunt around our tiny-ass trailer. "No estás loca," Mom said. "Estás pendeja!"

Still, my mom would often tell me she felt bad for my aunt. "Está enferma," she'd explain. "She has a hard life." I knew this had to be true because of the way she layered her cardigans on her delicate body. At first I thought my aunt, who is naturally pretty, was being modest. It wasn't until I started noticing the bruises on her arms and wrists and the way she tugged at her sleeves uncomfortably that I began to put two and two together.

I'd seen my uncle try to put one over on my parents, avoiding rent payments with elaborate and nonsensical excuses, but those fights were different than the ones between my mom and my tía. They didn't entertain me—they made me worry. Faces got too close and spit was always flying. Even as a five-year-old, I knew my uncle was worse to my aunt than to anyone else. She was quiet in his presence, submissive to his demands. "You're worthless," he'd yell, reminding her that she belonged to him. When my cousin got sick and threw up one day, my uncle grabbed my aunt by the hair, squeezing her curls in his hand and pushing her face into the vomit. "Clean," he ordered. She squirmed, struggling to do as she was told. I watched my mom's face get red-hot, flushed with anger and resentment. "No man has a right to do shit like that," she said. But she knew better than to get involved in the moment. She'd try to talk with my aunt when my uncle wasn't around, but my aunt wasn't able to leave him, no matter what he did to her.

After each fight, each beating, we'd watch my uncle try to play everything off. He'd spoil my aunt with gifts and clothes, recklessly spending money they didn't have. My aunt giggled from the attention, waving bags of clothes in front of us. I wondered if it was easy to forget bruises when they were hidden underneath Chanel foundation.

Before we lived together, I'd seen my tío Miguel as a good uncle, one we could take fun family trips with. Now I was embarrassed to be related to someone so angry, violent, and cruel. I couldn't bring myself to greet him, much less look him in the eye. He didn't deserve my attention. I didn't want to call him my tío. He didn't deserve to have a niece or a family. He didn't deserve respect. Sometimes I wondered if my aunt and my cousins would be better off without him. I fantasized about what would happen if he died in a car crash.

Living with my uncle and aunt also quickly taught me that there were people who couldn't be trusted. It was obvious that my parents didn't trust them. They did things to protect me from them all the time. At night, I slept in the same room as my parents, away from the pink room with green carpets in the middle of the trailer they'd decorated for me to have. "The room is too close to the kitchen," Mom said to my dad. "If she leaves the stove on, the first thing that will catch on fire is the wall next to her room."

"You're right," Dad said, shaking his head. "We should take her to the movie theater with us. She can't stay home alone."

"Sí," Mom replied. "She's safer with us."

Nothing put me to sleep quicker than the distant hum of the vacuum or my dad's popcorn leaf blower. But sometimes, after Mom and Dad tucked me in on my bench, I'd pry my eyes open and coax myself awake. I'd walk sleepily to the bathroom, to the end of the long halls. I'd paw through the lost and found, and eventually I would always find my way to my favorite spot: the concession stand. I'd stare at the locked glass cases full of vibrant packs of Skittles, Twizzlers, and enticing bars of chocolate, wondering how I could break in. I imagined myself turning on the popcorn machine and filling up a bag. But it was the one place my parents' key didn't allow us into. Management was protecting their sweet margins and savory revenue from the threat of their janitors; from the threat of me.

After a while, my parents stopped trying to coax me back to sleep. They figured I'd get tired eventually, and usually they were right. But while I was awake, I reveled in the novelty of an empty movie theater. I felt special there, like it belonged to me, like I got a chance to see this place in ways no one else ever could. The lights were dimmed, and everything was cast in blue shadows. The dirty carpets, the ceilings—everything was blue except for the stark white bathrooms my mom kept sparkling clean. I'd wander through the blue, slightly spooked, often feeling tingles of fear and excitement run down my back like electricity. I'd *slowly* turn around to see if anyone was following. Ghosts, figures, shadows. Anything was possible in an empty theater.

When I got too scared, I listened for the hum of the vacuum or the noise of the leaf blower and let it guide me to my parents. Often I'd find my dad and follow him like a lost puppy until I finally got too tired and had to curl up in the theater seats. Staring at the black screen, I let my mind fill the darkness with moving images in bright colors as if I was telling myself bedtime stories. Scarlet macaws soared through the space of my mind, dodging the monkeys in the trees trying to ground them. The birds would find their way through the lush rainforest until they were safely in their nest, high above the danger, hidden in the greens of the trees. Sometimes, my dad would unknowingly interrupt my silent movies and hand me a pair of sunglasses that somebody had dropped under the seat. I'd put them on and pretend to be famous. When Dad was finished cleaning, he'd come and pick up my sleeping body, cradling me safely in his arms.

"Papa, can we come in the day and watch a movie?" I'd ask in a whisper, still half-asleep. "Luego te traigo, mija. Later we will."

In a couple of hours, I'd have to wake up for school. Though usually focused in the classroom, I'd occasionally find myself thinking back to the movie theater, staring at the colorful posters on the wall, imagining them coming to life like I did on blank screens.

3

LITTLE BONES

I had just started first grade when I found out that my mom was going to have another baby.

"Elizabeth, escucha," she coaxed as I woke up one morning before school. "Vas a tener un hermanito!"

My jaw dropped, exposing the huecos I had from missing baby teeth. "Are you *serious*?" I didn't know what to expect or what exactly her being pregnant would mean for all of us. I knew only that a little *something* would be growing slowly in my mom's belly.

"I think it's going to be a boy," Mom replied with a smile.

———————

Mrs. C, my librarian at school, had recommended that I start reading the Magic Tree House books after seeing the stacks that I checked out weekly. They were chapter books, and I was excited to finally move on to more challenging texts.

Before long, I was engulfed in the stories of two siblings—a brother and a sister—as they went on adventures that crossed space and time. I craved a sibling that I could do the same with, somebody who would understand me and our family, who'd take on the world with me and whom I could take care of. I also wanted someone to boss around.

When Mom revealed that I would in fact soon have a little brother, it was the happiest day of my life. From that day forward, all I could think about was being a big sister. I spouted out names, trying to help my parents decide on one. At yard sales, I'd look for toys that I could give to my little brother. At one sale, I found a small knitted stuffed bear that reminded me of the little bear from the children's book *Corduroy*. It was perfect, soft, and clean. I carried it around with me as if it was my brother, imagining all the ways I would take care of him.

My mom got pregnant a little less than a year after she started working at the movie theater. Once she found out, she didn't stop or slow down; she kept cleaning toilets and floors, her belly slowly reaching toward the ground. Then people started visiting our trailer to check in on her. First it was my godparents from South Tucson, el tío Fauso and la tía Alicia, who hugged and congratulated my parents. My grandparents on my dad's side came afterwards, and their visits were always an ordeal. They didn't seem to care about our cramped living spaces; they simply claimed the room my parents and I shared. It didn't matter that it would result in the displacement of my waddling mother. On the other hand, I remembered, my tía Rocio and tío Miguel never offered their own space, and my grandparents never attempted to take it. "Your uncle inherited his mother's sense of entitlement," Mom would whisper to me. "He thinks he's their golden child." Wide-eyed, I'd nod, trying to figure out what the word *entitlement* even meant.

Although my mom seemed highly irritated by my grandparents' visit, I was excited. When they approached the sliding door on our trailer, my grandpa's crinkled smile lit up my eyes. He wasn't a particularly tall man, but he had a strong and imposing look to him. My grandma stood behind him, with freshly dyed jet-black hair a contrast to her fair skin. If it wasn't for a frown that seemed permanent, she even would've looked pretty.

"Qué no nos vas a saludar?" he asked.

Arms wide, I'd run up to them for a hug and a kiss, enveloping myself in their smell of expired Chanel No. 5. In the mornings that followed, I would jump onto my abuelo Marcelino's lap.

"Tell me stories about Puebla," I pleaded. "Tell me about my great-great-grandparents." I waited intently for him to set up scenes for me. My grandpa used language like a writer, filling my mind with images of his dilapidated childhood home, the dry landscape of el campo, and the strict and abusive behavior of his father. My grandpa was always honest, never shying away from the details that others usually hid from children.

"Tú tienes suerte, mija," he said. "I spent my childhood working, with only scraps to eat. All you have to worry about is school." Day by day I took in the stories of his youth and filled in bits and pieces of my grandfather's past.

"One time I did a full day of yard work," he said with a laugh.

"The old hag who hired me gave me a single avocado for my payment."

My grandpa also liked talking about philosophy, the origin of mankind, and the faults of religion. "Religious fanatics are the reason that there is so much human suffering," he said and sighed. Sometimes I didn't understand what he was talking about, but I always listened. His deep voice was full of life and wisdom.

My abuela Delia sometimes listened, too, but she always seemed irritated by his stories. "There you go with your sermons," she huffed. My grandmother seemed to resent the attention my grandpa received and the way people always stopped and listened to him. It was typical of her to interrupt and redirect the conversations back to her. But all she ever talked about were her aches and pains, and nobody wanted to listen to her endless complaints. Worst of all was the way my grandma sulked in a passive-aggressive fashion.

"Oh, you know we ran out of groceries back in Mexico. I wish we had someone who could take us to Walmart," she would say. If her sulking didn't work, she'd pinch her face at anything that displeased her before demanding to be driven to Walmart and the mall. She *knew* she was a guest, and she expected to be treated as one. Somehow a trip to one store would inevitably devolve into a full day at Ross and TJ Maxx. She always got her way, and my mom was the one who ended up chauffeuring her around as Abuelo Marcelino followed along.

My grandparents expected more out of my mother than out of any of my uncles' wives. It was as if they sensed her rebellious nature, her disgust at being seen as *just* a housewife, and her displeasure at having to take care of them. More than anything, it displeased them that she spoke her mind and openly disagreed with their often narrow-minded opinions.

Still, Mom held her own, setting as many boundaries as she could.

"Don't you dare think that I'll be cooking lunch and breakfast for them," she said to my dad. "Your brother can do his part and take them out." My dad would nod in agreement, exasperated. "I feel like I'm being put between a wall and a knife," he replied.

When my grandparents were around, Tío Miguel turned into even more of a pompous asshole, kissing up to them while doing none of the hosting. The last straw for my mom was when my uncle talked down as if she belonged to him.

"Can't you see that she needs someone to drive her around? Do as my mother says," he demanded.

Seething, Mom snapped back. "Tú no eres nadie para dar órdenes. This type of shit may work for your wife, but it sure as hell won't work for me." Unable to come up with a good response, my uncle stormed off, yelling obscenities as he closed the door to his room.

Even when my mom agreed to help out and take my grandparents around town for errands, they still found ways to convey their disappointment. They openly scoffed at my mom and dad for working nights at the theater as janitors. "We used to rub alcohol on our hands before carrying you," my grandma would throw out. "Now you clean toilets."

Mom bit her lip, holding herself back from saying anything.

"She's old school," Dad said. "I've tried and I can't make them change."

Mom ignored his excuses. As a kid, I had never known my dad to be afraid of things, but I had always known he was scared of disappointing his parents. Cleaning popcorn and gum off the floor wasn't anyone's dream job, but I never saw their hard work as a reason to feel ashamed. I loved being at the theater with them, and together, my parents made enough money to keep us afloat, pay our bills, and even attempt to save a little to create a small safety net for our growing family. They did not, however, make enough to send extra money to my abuela Delia and abuelo Marcelino.

So like the rest of Dad's siblings, my parents began to lie about how much money they had. If my grandparents found out that my parents had more money—if they saw Mom with nice clothes or a new purse—they'd demand it for their ranch back in Mexico. As their eldest son, my dad seemed nearly incapable of refusing his parents. My grandparents knew this and leached off him despite knowing full well that it caused conflict between my parents. At night, when my mom and dad thought I was fast asleep, I'd hear them argue in whispers. Whispers, after all, were how we got our information.

———————

Toward the end of my grandparents' stay, my mom was feeling more fatigued than ever. To make up for it, my dad took over more of her work at the theater, so that she only had to show up in the early morning to clean the bathrooms and windows when management came to check in on the workers.

"If they find out you're not coming in at all, they'll fire you," Dad warned. "We have to make it seem like we're both doing all the work, not just me." Mom agreed, aware that the movie theater would be happy to pay one laborer instead of two for the same amount of work. Management wouldn't hesitate to exploit the situation.

I watched my parents try to get into a new rhythm while my grandparents continued to observe, with no signs that they were thinking of departing. My parents didn't take me to the movie theater while my grandparents were around—instead, I waited for them to come home. At around 4:30 A.M., Dad would sneak in quietly, gently kissing my forehead before showering and hopping into bed. My mom would usually stay behind at the theater and finish up what my dad hadn't been able to. From the pullout bed in the living room, I'd sit up and wait for her, unable to fall back asleep on the mattress's hard springs. When Mom got in, she smiled at me. "Duérmete! You have to go to school soon!"

In the early morning darkness, I grinned back at her as I covered myself with the blanket and she slid in next to me. A couple of hours later, I felt Dad's gentle nudge. "Let's get ready," he said, "so that your mom can sleep in."

From the corner of my eye, I caught my grandma's figure entering the living room. I watched her stare at my mom under the blankets and then look toward me and my dad.

"Buenos días," he said.

"She should be up and getting your daughter ready," she replied harshly. "You're doing a woman's job. Are you not a man?"

Quietly Dad turned away from his mother, and in an instant, I felt his tenderness disappear as he ordered me around. "Apúrate, ya metete a bañar," he demanded.

I don't know what woke my mom up that day. I don't know if I talked back to my dad or if I cried. I must have. I must have told him to stop being mean, to stop holding my arm so tightly as he led me to the shower. What I do know is that my dad yelled at my mom when she showed up behind him, asking him what was wrong.

"Vete de aquí!" he yelled. "I can do this on my own!"

"Stop being so rough with her," Mom pleaded. "You're yelling."

What happened next was a blur. One second, I saw my mom, standing strong and rigid. "Come here," she ushered me.

As I moved closer to her, Dad continued his argument. "I can handle it!" he screamed. "Get out of the way!"

I watched as he roughly shoved my mom, making her fall backward into the tub. I screamed as she tried to stand up, still in the ratty shirt she'd worn to work, while holding her belly that cradled my baby brother. Without thinking, I began to run up to her, but my dad pushed me back.

"Stay out of it," he said sternly as I slumped onto the floor. Silently I watched my mother get herself up as Dad slowly started coming back to his senses. He didn't say anything as Mom picked me up. We gathered our things, and as we walked out of the house, I noticed my grandparents sitting at the kitchen table. They didn't say a word. They didn't intervene.

Calmly, Mom buckled me into the back seat of the car and drove us to the nearest gas station, where I watched her dial 911 through the window.

She was safe.

I was safe.

And the dream of adventures with my little brother was still alive in her belly.

───────────

I remember having recurring dreams of my dad getting hand-cuffed. He was wearing a black shirt, the same black shirt he always wore. The black shirt he bought in bulk from Banana Republic because he liked how it fit. The one he wore when he volunteered as a chaperone for school field trips. I could almost feel his sweat build up and soak through his shirt as faceless officers led him away. In the background, I saw my grandparents. My grandma, crying. My grandpa, rigid.

Every time I woke up, I'd remember the aftermath of their fight, my nightmare turned reality. Dad was released the same day and agreed to go to anger management courses. Mom didn't pursue any legal action—instead, she let her silence speak for her. When my mom wasn't in the room, my grandma turned to me and said, "You know, it is your mom's fault that your dad got arrested. It is a miracle that he wasn't deported."

I never acknowledged my grandparents when they told me this or when they finally left a couple of days later. Instead, I sat at the kitchen table—in the same way that they did—pretending I couldn't hear them.

4

HEARTBEAT

My mother's body when she was almost eight months pregnant looked unnatural to my seven-year-old eyes, her thin twiggy legs and frame somehow carrying an enormous round belly. At that point, my mom really couldn't work, so she stayed home. At night, while my dad went to work, I'd lie by Mom's side and tap it like Dad did to watermelons at the supermarket, listening to see if they were ripe. We were sure the baby would be big and healthy.

Against all my pleading, my parents had settled on naming the baby Fernando—the same name that the class clown had in first grade. Despite hating his name, I couldn't wait to meet my brother.

One night right after dusk, before my dad left for work, my mom went outside to fetch the laundry from the clothesline. There had been construction earlier in the day on some underground pipelines running through the yard. After hours, the crew had precariously left bricks and piping scattered throughout. It was dark and Mom never saw the piles of bricks; she only felt their impact on her belly after she fell. She sat on the ground for a while, holding her stomach before wiping the blood from her knees. As she hobbled back inside the trailer, she began to worry. She went to the bathroom and stared at the blood at the bottom of the toilet and stood still as her water broke. I stared at her from the doorway, watching her careful movements and her face contort.

"I have to go to the hospital," she told my dad.

Later at the hospital, my godparents from South Tucson, el tío Fausto and la tía Alicia, picked me up. It didn't matter that my tío Miguel and tía Rocio were back at the trailer—I wasn't to be left with them. Instead, I spent that night with my godparents, watching TV, playing Grand Theft Auto, and eating Rice Krispies with two spoonfuls of sugar sprinkled on top. By the time my mom was taken in and evaluated, it was too late to try to stop early labor. She was fully dilated, and there was no stopping Fernando. As the night nurse explained the urgency of the situation, my dad promptly gathered his things and prepared to leave the room. The nurse sternly pulled him back in.

"Sir, you're going to have to help me, I don't have four hands," she said as she pulled an alarm. Dad was directed to hold back one of Mom's legs as the room filled up with nurses and doctors.

My brother was taken away as soon as he was born, his little body quickly examined by the neonatal intensive care unit (NICU) team. He was premature, his lungs underdeveloped.

Fernando was stabilized and put under the same lights I'd been put under after getting jaundice, a tiny sleep mask placed over his wrinkled face. When my mom and dad were finally allowed to enter the NICU, they were surrounded by tiny hands, little feet, and anxiety-ridden parents. They walked by babies so small they could fit in the palm of your hands, babies indistinguishable under masks, tubes, and IVs. When they finally reached my brother, they felt relief. He was plump and round, with pale skin—the perfect American baby—and the NICU nurses were optimistic and enchanted by the strength of his heartbeat.

The next morning, el tío Fausto woke me up to share the news of my brother's birth. I was so excited that I fell back, my small legs extended joyfully in the air. Throughout the day, I constantly asked when I would be able to see Fernando.

"Ten paciencia," my uncle and aunt said, emphasizing that I should be patient and appeasing me with more sugary cereal. After what felt like forever, Dad and Mom, who had been discharged, picked me up. Fernando, they informed me, was still at the hospital as they examined his development. I was finally on my way to meet my little brother.

Together, my parents and I walked through the automatic sliding glass doors and the hallways of the clinic, which were bustling with activity. I was intrigued by every person and everything we passed as we made our way to the small room made for nursing NICU mothers. There, the nurses handed my brother to my mother for breastfeeding. I stared at his wrinkled pale face and reddish-brown hair.

"He looks like you," I told Mom as I delicately put my hand on the pastel blue blanket he was wrapped in. My dad, prepared with a disposable camera, told us to smile. As the camera flashed, I hoped that it would capture my excitement. Finally I'd have someone to share the world with.

For the next sixteen days, my brother was in the NICU under the careful watch of nurses. "He looks normal," I said to my mom.

"Yes, but his lungs needed more time," she replied. I struggled to understand why we couldn't simply bring Fernando home. He wasn't as small as the other babies in the NICU—he was thick, his rolls visible when he was held. But the nurses were right: his lungs were weak, and although they'd mitigated most of the damage from his premature birth, they predicted that his lungs might be compromised for the rest of his life.

During this time, Mom and Dad had to quickly recover and go back to work at the movie theater. Every day after school, they picked me up and we'd go visit my brother, where my mom would try to feed him. When he refused, Mom rolled her eyes and mumbled, "Those nurses must've already fed him." I laughed, adjusting myself next to her, trying to find Fernando's distinguishing features, imagining what he might look like once he grew. He was so small. All I wanted to do was to protect him.

When Fernando was finally released from the NICU, the bill my parents received in the mail a few days later startled them. It was for over fifty thousand dollars. They had no medical benefits, no insurance, and the management at the theater had been delaying their pay, some months skipping it altogether. My mom and dad discussed what had to be done while continuing to work.

For a few months, we all went back to the movie theater every night, even Fernando. Armed with his stroller and with a fierce desire to take care of my brother just like he was one of my dolls, I'd walk up and down the shadowed hallways of the movie theater, pushing and pulling him along. Squished next to him in the stroller was the bear I'd found at the yard sale. The darkness still scared me, but it was better when I had Fernando to battle the world with me.

The hospital bills and the infrequent pay from the movie theater was making things complicated. "They owe us for more than two months of work," Dad told Mom. "You have to do something about it," she encouraged. "You're the one that tried studying law anyway."

Whenever I heard my dad talking about money, I thought about the management team running the movie theater, businesspeople doing nothing but crunching numbers. They outsourced the cleaning services to other companies, often shady ones that hired contract workers—people like my parents. The big movie theater chains of the world didn't care if those contract workers were undocumented or if they lacked basic human rights like insurance and healthcare. They didn't care if the companies skipped their payments. It was easy to overlook. Overlooking reality is cheap. My dad knew this and decided to beat them at their own game. He decided to make them rethink what *cheap labor* was capable of.

At work, he finally persuaded one of the managers at the movie theater to give him the contractor's number. He wanted to talk to the headquarters, and his managers had avoided for months giving my dad any contact information. They knew he wasn't getting paid—even his minuscule wage—but raising their voices was too much of a risk.

Our trailer had a phone stuck to the wall. I watched Dad pick it up, standing rigidly as he curled the black cord around his finger, which grew purple from constriction. He was so angry that he spoke clearly and concisely in English. I noticed the muscles around his jaw tensing as he spoke sternly into the receiver. I recognized his anger in myself sometimes. The way I sometimes couldn't control it. The tight way I held my teeth together whenever I disagreed with someone or felt wronged. Though my dad's outbursts scared me, I was proud of the ways he stood against injustice.

"Now you listen," he yelled into the receiver, punching every word, "if you don't pay me, I *will* be taking legal action. You will be hearing from my lawyer shortly." On the other end, the businesspeople crunched numbers. They weighed the cost of the situation, of getting discovered for their shady employment practices.

Management didn't know what I did: that sometimes fear and anger feel similar. They didn't know that there was an uncontrolled fire fueling Dad from the *inside*. They thought he was stupid, incapable, powerless against the system.

"Sir, now hold on," the woman replied on the other end. "I'm sending two men from Phoenix down to Tucson right now with a check. Can you wait?"

In the next few days, riding the wave of empowerment, my

dad got a lawyer. It was the same lawyer that every Latino used—famous for his commercials in Spanish, which were blasted out over the radio. He sued the construction workers who left the bricks in our yard, and he won. He let *them* pay the fifty-thousand-dollar hospital bill from my brother's premature birth. But not a penny more.

Fernando's lungs were still weak. He would have asthma for the rest of his life.

The lawyer told my dad, "We can ask for more money."

Dad refused. "I'm not that kind of person."

Afterwards, Dad began taking me to the movie theater—not just during the night shift, but also to *see* the movies. But instead of paying for tickets, he waited for the right moment and pulled me into a large crowd of people, my heart racing, so we could sneak through unnoticed. There was no way my dad would be giving a cent of his money back to the company that too often had tried to stiff him. Instead, we would steal a little bit back. After all, we were used to making ourselves invisible.

Once we were seated, Dad would pull out a can of Coca-Cola and some chips he'd hidden in the pockets of his jacket. I was used to the sight of movie posters outside every viewing room of the theater, but once I was actually able to watch the films, I was dazzled as the characters from the posters came to life on the screen. I experienced magic, watching wizards soar on broomsticks. And like so many times before, I felt safe with my dad in the blue darkness of the theater. The two of us unseen; this time I was a ghost, and he was a shadow.

5

A DIFFERENT NAME

After my mom had my brother and management finally noticed she'd stopped coming in as much, she was fired. My dad was left with twice the work but half the income, exactly what they had always feared. When Dad would come home, he'd spend the rest of the day walking with a slight hunch, taking tiny steps from our room at the end of the trailer to the bathroom down the hallway. He had recently turned forty and his curly jet-black hair had started to gray around his side-burns.

"Que viejito te ves, Papá," I said and smirked.

"Old man? What are you talking about? I look great," he replied with a smile. Sometimes he'd grunt and lie down on the floor, staring up at the ceiling, to make the back pain go away. Fernando, still a small toddler, would curl up next to him. I would follow, both of us resting under Dad's arms as he held us close.

———————

Dad's back pain subsided when he quit working at the movie theater less than a year later. At first I wasn't worried about how our family would make money—Dad was always good at finding ways; he was entrepreneurial and often had savvy business ideas. In his head, he'd quickly make estimates of how much he would need to invest in something for it to turn a profit, discarding ideas that he considered flops. My dad couldn't go to a steakhouse without thinking that he could do it better, scoffing at how the cooks burnt ridges on the meat purely for *looks* when they needed to do it for taste. He couldn't go to the grocery store without identifying something missing from the shelves, focusing in particular on the quality of flour tortillas sold commercially. In Mexico, flour tortillas were delicate, even flaky, when put on the stove. They weren't like the rubbery ones sold at Walmart and certainly nothing like the ones white people use to make giant burritos.

Still, there was always an undercurrent of *if* lingering in our financial situation that made it hard to feel secure and be able to move forward. *If* my grandparents hadn't depleted our savings when we came to the United States, my dad might have been able to start a business, build a restaurant, or simply have had a head start. *If* my parents had citizenship, then they would have been able to get good jobs and save. *If* we didn't buy clothes at Banana Republic or Gap, then maybe we would have had enough money to rent our own place. We were always short of something and there was always somebody to blame.

So my dad had to work with what he had. All our cars were salvaged from subastas—auctions held in lots where insurance companies sent cars that they considered totaled. Dad had a good eye for finding ones that could be fixed up, and he'd place a reasonable bid. For $600, he'd buy a car. For another $200 he'd buy the broken parts. He knew someone in South Tucson who would cut him a deal and paint the car, making it good as new. If he got lucky, he could sell it for $5,000.

On weekends, I'd go with my dad to the subastas. They weren't too far from our house, only a three-minute drive up the road that led to the Rillito River crossing. The subastas reminded me of cemeteries—there was a place for the rich and the poor. You could find all sorts of cars there, from the most current and sleek Mercedes-Benz to an old rusty station wagon that was probably named Betsy by its previous owner. They didn't normally allow kids, but Dad snuck me in—something I was becoming more accustomed to—and told me to be careful. Our feet would crunch through the gravel and sparse weeds. I watched for snakes and scorpions hiding in the shadows, cooling off from the grueling heat. We'd open car doors and look inside, finding half-eaten Snickers bars melted into cup holders, forgotten toys and baby rattles. Sometimes our finds were more interesting. Among the loose change and sunglasses, my dad found expensive pens with French names. "Se llaman Montblanc," Dad would say. "I'll add it to my collection."

I enjoyed following him around as he circled cars. He was logical and good at making quick, accurate judgments. "This damage is only surface level," he'd say in reference to a big Sequoia. "What do you think about us taking this one home?"

While my mom was good at finding Burberry at the thrift store, my dad was good at spotting things that people wouldn't bid too much on. Eventually I learned to spot Subarus, Toyotas, and Nissans and determine their quality.

"These Japanese cars are reliable," he told me.

"Alice's parents drive a Chevy," I'd reply, referring to a car I'd seen my classmate step into after school.

"Well, American cars are shit," he'd say with a laugh. Bumpers, fenders, and hoods were always easy to replace. He looked for clean interiors and told me that the cleaner the car, the better it was probably taken care of. He talked about the number of cylinders each motor had and how efficient on gas they would be.

Eventually I got bored with his car knowledge and would dream about what I wanted to have one day. "I want a red Jeep with a hard hood, but I'd settle for a black one if I had to." Jeeps showed up at the car yard every so often, but they always sold high once auctioned.

"Nah, Jeeps are hard to handle and not the most comfortable," Dad would warn. "I'll get you a BMW instead. People are always crashing their BMWs."

———————

The money we earned from the subastas was the opposite of steady—unpredictable and time-consuming, they didn't provide a safety net. My dad would fix cars and wait weeks for them to sell. Sometimes he'd have to drive to Mexico to drop it off with potential buyers. On these trips, my grandparents cornered him into giving them money.

"Rubén, we need money for the ranch," they said. They tried to tie him down, reminding him that he had responsibilities in Mexico. When Dad came back to Arizona with less money than expected, my mom short-circuited and lost her mind at the ways he was so easily manipulated.

"Eliza, you have to understand," he began. Quickly she cut him off, frustrated.

"Y nosotros *qué*? What about your family here? What about your children?"

Eventually Dad was able to find a job at a thrift store where he was paid under the table. Having been to the thrift store tons of times on family trips, I laughed at the thought of my dad's stocking used clothing. I couldn't picture him sorting it by size, gently placing each item on a hanger, and then color-coordinating it on the racks. In some ways, I even felt like it was too delicate a task—too *feminine*—to be his job. The reality was that Dad was usually sent to the back rooms of the store. Somehow that felt more fitting to me, as he had always been good at keeping out of sight.

My classmates also weren't rich, or at least I didn't think so. What I did know was that *we* were poor. Beyond the obvious fact that we lived in a shared trailer in a mobile home park south of the river, my parents had literally been janitors, getting paid crumbs under the table. After a few rounds of getting bullied by the popular kids at school, I realized that I could use this "poor girl" narrative to my advantage. At sleepovers that I had been invited to as an afterthought, I'd casually drop the fact that I slept on a mattress laid on the floor around eavesdropping parents.

"Yeah, we all have to sleep in one room," I'd say to my wide-eyed audience. Over time, I found that telling people bits and pieces of my reality made people react. Smugly, I'd watch people contort uncomfortably, thinking of what to say.

"Oh, but you're so well mannered," some parents would say, as if being poor meant that I couldn't be polite. Sometimes I was met with resistance to what I considered a fact.

"How can you be poor if you wear stuff from the Gap?" my classmates would ask.

"I guess you've never heard of *sales*," I'd reply. "It's too bad you know nothing about style."

Mom and Dad caught on to my act after my classmate Alice's parents stopped by. In the past, they'd taken me to church with them. They were *super* Christian, the kind that had cringey bands singing songs about Jesus during mass. Shyly they knocked on our front door.

"Hi, we thought we'd drop off some clothes we had," they chirped. "We figured you might need it more than us." From the couch, I watched my mom hold in a gasp, quickly putting her hand to her face.

"Gracias, gracias," she replied, unsure of what to do.

"We're happy to be able to support the community," they replied. As soon as they left, I knew that I was screwed.

"Oh my god, Elizabeth!" Mom yelled. "What did you tell them?!"

My dad, nearly crying in laughter, added, "Do you realize we're not even *that poor*? I bet you we have a better TV than they do." Giggling, I shrugged them off.

"Wasn't that TV broken when we got it, though?" I quipped as my mom picked up a heavy pleather jacket from the donation box.

"I would never be caught wearing this," Mom said. "Poor or not, at least we have taste." I nodded in agreement, finally feeling

a bit of the embarrassment my parents felt. Despite our resourcefulness, we made an effort to look put together. More than that,
we were fashionable in a way that you might not expect someone
to be in the poor immigrant neighborhoods we lived in. Belts
matched shoes. Shirts were ironed. Our shit might have been
from the racks or the thrift store, but we knew cashmere and silk
when we felt it. Maybe it was because my parents understood that
looking a certain way could open doors. As I looked at the box of
clothes my friend's parents had dropped off, I imagined myself
as a city girl with a nice watch, sunglasses, and a bag just like my
mom's. In my head, I didn't look poor.

Even though I had a hard time making friends at school, I
knew that I always had a friend waiting for me back home.
I'd met Kayla the week after we first moved into the trailer, when
I didn't know any English. I was busy playing with dolls when I
heard a confident knock on the glass door. Outside stood a little
girl with bright red hair, waving frantically.

"Hi, do you want to come out to play?" she asked. Confused,
I looked toward my dad, who had been changing the channels
mindlessly on the TV.

"Elizabeth, quiere jugar. I think she wants you to go play
with her." Cautiously I moved to the door, where I noticed a big
gap in Kayla's smile and a doll hanging loosely in her hand.
Turns out we didn't need a common language to play Barbie.

As I learned English, Kayla and I became BFFs. We solidi-
fied our friendship with matching plastic heart necklaces and
a secret language that only we could understand. Day after day,

I would knock on the neighbor's door, asking Kayla's grandparents if she was over. Before long, I found out that Kayla lived on the opposite side of the trailer park with her mom and dad, both smokers with harsh and raspy voices. My parents trusted Kayla, and at some point they let me wander off to go visit her.

Kayla's trailer had a lot more stuff than ours did. Hanging from their porch were dozens of wind chimes and dream catchers with bleached white feathers flowing in the wind. Everywhere I looked there seemed to be little piles of clutter. Trinkets, mini statues, and eclectic rocks. Enthusiastically Kayla ushered me inside.

"This is my mom and my sheltie. Her name is Cassie," she said as I walked into the darkness of their living room.

"Hi," added her mom while gently petting the dog. "I have a migraine, but you girls run along." Kayla's mom was thin and so tanned that it made her wrinkles stand out, and I wondered if that's why she kept the curtains drawn. Next to her spot on the couch I observed a small table full of the exact same trinkets that were everywhere else. On her lap was a pile of scratch-off lottery tickets.

"One time she won five hundred dollars!" Kayla squealed. Hearing the commotion, Kayla's dad walked up to meet us. He was huge—if I hadn't known he was Kayla's dad, I would've kept my distance.

"My name's Gar," he rumbled. "Imma call you Lizzy if you don't mind." Kayla and I both laughed.

"Your dad looks like a southern Captain Hook." I giggled.

"He *wishes* he had as much hair," she replied. Gar's hair was long and trailed down his back in a ponytail, gray with split ends. Across his head was a bandanna that hid his bald spot.

When Gar was in a good mood, he'd take us on rides in his old blue Ford truck. But sometimes Gar wasn't. Like the time a part on his Harley stopped working that he couldn't fix. I got the feeling that he was prone to outbursts like my dad was and wondered if all dads were slightly neurotic. One thing Kayla and I knew for sure was to keep our distance from Gar whenever he was tinkering with his motorcycle, because then he hated to be bothered. Kayla's parents were hard-core Harley-Davidson lovers. To me, that made them feel extra American, and when you put them next to Kayla, a girl with bright red hair who wore pink shirts and dresses, it made me smile. Despite how rough they looked on the outside, it was clear Kayla was their baby girl.

My parents liked Kayla even though they didn't like tattoos or the smell of cigarettes, and I felt pride in finally having someone like her to confide in. I didn't have that with any of the kids at school. None of them understood like Kayla did. I didn't need to tell her that we were poor or explain my crowded living situation. Together, we existed in a world we both knew. We brushed each other's hair and pressed on fake tattoos that I'd have to scrub off before running home.

When Dad lost his job at the thrift store, Kayla was the only person I ever told. He began to spend his days fixing up cars, returning only to eat his dinner in silence. For weeks, he had nothing to say.

"My dad's sad about not having a job," I sighed to Kayla.

"Why do adults even want to work so much?" she asked with a cautious smile. Quietly we both sat on the swing sets, kicking up sand with our feet. We both knew what it was like when money was low. As the sun went down, Kayla perked up. "You should come over for dinner tonight!" she said and smiled. "I'll tell my dad to make us Hot Pockets."

I wrinkled my nose in disgust. "You need to try other things," I replied.

"Shut up, I'll race you there," she said.

At dinner, Kayla told Gar about how my dad had lost his job. "Aw, Lizzy, don't worry about that," Gar encouraged. "I think I have something up my sleeve that can fix this all up. I'll talk to him when I drop you off after dinner."

Eyes wide, I nodded, unsure if I had overshared another detail that would embarrass my parents. True to his word, Gar dropped me off later that night and started a conversation with my dad, putting his arm over his shoulder like they were bros. From the corner of my eye, I watched them shoot the shit, Dad laughing and speaking in broken English. When he finally walked back inside the house, there was a smile on his face.

"Dice Gar que tiene trabajo," he said. "The factory that he works in needs new workers." There was a sense of relief as he told us. Arms wide, Dad picked me up, twirling me around like he had when I was little.

"Gracias, mija." His praise made what I had done feel useful. Somehow I felt like I was helping my family move forward.

The next day, Dad met Gar outside a warehouse full of machinery and dust. "This is it: Square Corp," he announced.

When my dad inhaled, the air tasted like metal. "Como sabor a sangre," he'd later tell me. "Like the taste of blood."

After a quick tour of the equipment, a manager named Steve came up to him with some paperwork. On the documents were a list of the potential risks one could be faced with by working in that particular environment.

"You'll be working with chrome," said Steve. "I can't imagine you know what that is, but it's no bueno," he continued.

Dad ignored Steve's shitty accent as he read over the text, taking note of the fine print in the same way he'd done in college before dropping out. "I studied to be a lawyer," he replied. "I know what this means."

. . . nasal septum ulcerations and perforations . . .

Steve chuckled at my dad's response. "That doesn't matter here in America," he said, snickering. As machines whizzed in the background, Dad realized why they hadn't asked any questions about his background. This was a job that nobody else wanted.

. . . liver, organ, and brain damage, lung cancer . . .

Quietly my dad signed the paper and handed it back to Steve. "Edgar López Cruz," Steve read as he glanced over the document. "You can start tomorrow."

From then on, Gar and everyone at work called my dad Edgar. Later, when I asked why they didn't call him by his real name, Dad simply said, "My real name doesn't matter here in America."

6

THE LITTLE HOUSE BY
THE FUNERAL HOME

I t was clear that my little brother Fernando was going to be a blunt little shit from the first moment that he started babbling. Fer, as I liked to call him, always said the first things that popped into his mind, especially during his terrible twos.

"I'm milk like mom," he'd say with a straight face. "*You*— well, you're chocolate like dad," he continued as he eyed me up and down from the comfort of my mom's arms.

"Ves, Mama, he's not innocent," I'd stammer back.

"No sabe lo que dice," Mom would reply. "He's only a baby." Fer was right, though. He was both lighter and less hairy than me, a fact that drove me crazy.

"I don't understand why *he* has blond hair that you can't see," I complained. "The doctor was right to call me a monkey!"

"Oh, stop," my dad interjected. "People would kill for your eyebrows." I rolled my eyes. I'd heard that lie for years growing up, making me believe that all adults were either blind or liars. "Mija, believe me," Dad continued. "You're beautiful like your mom."

My mom was absolutely drop-dead gorgeous. It was undeniable to anyone who met her.

At school, the popular girls would taunt me about it. "I can't believe that's *your* mom," they'd tease. "Are you sure you weren't adopted?"

Quickly I sneered back. "At least I'll look like her when I'm older. You guys might not get so lucky."

My classmates' moms reacted to mine in similar ways. "Oh, you can't speak English?" they asked, confused. "You look like a gringa, though!"

With ease, Mom dismissed them. "No, yo soy a hundred percent mexicana," she replied charmingly.

"Maybe they want to be your friends," I told Mom later.

Biting her lip, she tried to hold back a mischievous smile. "Recuerda, it's better to be alone than with bad company," she said. "Besides, I have you, mi chiquitita hermosa."

Before bed, Mom would tell Fer and me stories about her childhood in a small town on Mexico's Sonoran coastline. "When I was little, there were no hotels," she said, referencing the private beach clubs and four-star hotels that had taken over. "Peñasco wasn't *Rocky Point*—there were no tourists. It was a fisherman town, and your grandpa was a captain." She smiled. "My hair was super short, and my face was as round and as cute as yours," she continued while squishing my cheeks.

"Were you sad when my abuelo Chayo would go out fishing?" my brother asked.

"Siempre, I always clung to his leg trying to stop him from leaving," she said. "But he had a lot of mouths to feed." After all, we had watched my dad work overtime to keep us going, so it made sense that my abuelo Chayo had done the same.

My mom was the fifth child out of a total of seven, and unlike the rest of her siblings, she had freckles and straight red-brown hair that glowed like embers in the summer sun. When my grandmother carried her around town, people would gawk at the beautiful baby in her arms, equally enamored with her and curious as to why she didn't look like the rest of her siblings. But as she grew older, Mom didn't care what people thought. All she knew was that she lived in a house where everyone was family. Within the four walls of her childhood home, cousins, uncles, and the occasional stray dog all found themselves welcome.

"Why did you leave home so young?" I asked. "You were only fifteen."

"I moved to Caborca because there were better opportunities elsewhere," she said. "Besides, that's where I met your dad."

Caborca was only a two-hour drive away from Puerto Peñasco, my mother's home, but things were different there. There was only a stagnant dry heat—no ocean breezes to cool you down. My mom moved around from family member to family member, staying with la tía Lola for a year before eventually finding herself at my great-grandmother nana María's house, on the corner of Avenida 13 de Julio and la Calle Obregón. However, those in Caborca—the *locals*—knew where to find nana María if they wanted to. Nana María's house was simply the one next to the flower shop and the funeral home. The neighborhood was small, tightly knit. El tío Kala, who also lived in nana María's house, rode around on his bike greeting every person he passed by their first name.

While the house was small, Mom was warmly welcomed by nana María and el tío Kala. She shared a bed with her grandmother and enjoyed the simplicity of life, sitting outside with nana María and el tío Kala in the afternoons, watching the happenings at the funeral home and the flower shop.

"Who do you think died?" Mom whispered to nana María, who knew everything.

"Doña Julia's son," she replied. "Muy joven, what a tragedy." Together, they'd watch as cars slowly filed up the street. They weren't afraid of death, but they were curious and entertained by the grief, humor, and chaos of the funerals. There would be people crying, dancing, drinking, and eating. Each funeral brought with it unique family dynamics.

Other days were lighter, like Valentine's Day. My mom would walk by the flower shop idly, peeking in to see the young men of Caborca pick out roses and flowers. She judged them by the size of their bouquets, wondering who the lucky girl was. My mother often wondered if she'd like to receive flowers one day but was also torn by the fact that blossoms were bought for both the living and the dead.

My favorite stories about my mom's time with nana María involved magic. "Weird things happened while living with nana María," Mom would say. "Curious things." Night after night I begged her to tell me stories about the spirits that seemed to surround her.

"There was a time when a doll was left on the front door," Mom said one evening. "Nana María wasn't home, but when I got close, I noticed that it was full of tiny needles."

"What did you do?" I asked, eyes wide.

"I took the needles out," she explained. "Le estaban haciendo brujería, witchcraft." Apparently, nana María began an entire cleanse after the doll showed up, ushering spirits out of her house by cussing them out. "They're dead, but they're not deaf!" she exclaimed.

At first Mom had thought that the doll might have been a child's prank, but strange things kept happening. "One time, the dresses I had in my closet were completely slashed," she said. "There was nothing that could explain why or how it happened."

My favorite story, though, was the one about the black butterfly, when the most curious of things happened after my mom had come back from a party. Quietly she had walked past the sleeping nana María and el tío Kala, careful not to wake them. She slipped into the bathroom, which was lit up by a shrine to the Virgin Mary and a single bulb wired with an old Christmas light cable.

"The light was flickering when I saw it in the mirror," Mom began.

"What was it?" I pressed.

"It was a giant butterfly, but it was pitch black. I'd never seen something like that before!" After the butterfly fluttered toward her, my mom smacked it down with a flip-flop. The next day, as nana María prepared café de olla on the stove, Mom asked, "Nana, did you see the butterfly in the bathroom?"

Nana María's face was skeptical. "No, mija, what are you talking about?"

"Last night there was a black butterfly in the bathroom. I killed it before going to bed." Nana María turned off the stove and quickly scurried toward the bathroom as my mom followed.

"Are you sure you didn't dream it?" My mother shook her head, picking up the flip-flop she'd smacked it down with.

"Look, Nana," she said and pointed. Imprinted on the bottom of the flip-flop was a faint gray stain of a butterfly. Eyes wide, nana María began taking everything out of the bathroom in search of it. When it was clear that the butterfly was not there, nana María grabbed a bottle of holy water and sprayed it around the house.

"Es el diablo, mija," she said to my mother. "But he's not in charge here."

"Was everything okay after that?" I asked Mom.

"Yes, nothing happened." That night, nana María, el tío Kala, and my mother went to bed as music from the funeral home reached them through open windows. They fell asleep to the soft murmur of mourning women in prayer and the cackle of drunk men idling in the parking lot. Among the locals, my mother, nana María, and el tío Kala were known as the inseparable trio who lived in the curious little house by the funeral home.

Not long after Mom moved into nana María's house, she met my dad at a local dance and their whirlwind love story began. At first they went on drives around town after making a stop to pick up raspados, colorful shaved ice prepared with creams and all sorts of fresh fruits. My mom had found a job as a secretary, and every day after work, Dad would be there to pick her up. People noticed them together, watching as my dad showed off my mom. Eventually he brought her to his house for dinner to meet his parents, my abuela Delia and abuelo Marcelino, for the first time.

The inside of the Camarillo household was as elegant as

the outside. The traditional Spanish-style home had rooms with magnificently high ceilings. Graceful brick arches supported by thick wooden beams were in every room; the floor was covered with brand-new carpeting that extended up the stairway to the second floor. The house was so large that despite having furnishings and decor, it still felt empty. My mother noticed the way the curtains were drawn, blocking the light from the outside. *It would look better here with more light,* she thought.

El abuelo Marcelino was welcoming, greeting my mother as he would any new guest. With black hair like my father's but highlighted by streaks of silver, he had an imposing presence. He had grown up in Tehuacan, Puebla, in southern Mexico, where almost everyone had deep Indigenous roots. Any person who met him for the first time knew within minutes that he could silence a room, a skill he had learned after years of studying law and philosophy. Although my mother liked my grandfather right away, she was wary of him and his carefully political nature.

My abuela Delia, on the other hand, skirted my mom the first time they met, refusing to take her outstretched hand.

"My hands are wet," my grandmother told her, but Mom knew there was more to it than that. La abuela Delia was visibly fifteen years younger than my grandfather, a petite woman with fair skin and perfectly drawn eyebrows. It took only a few moments for Mom to gather herself and observe the dynamics at play: an overbearing father, a critical mother, a hesitant son. My dad, noticing the uneasiness in the room, quickly declared that it was time to sit down.

"Vamos a comer. Let's go eat," he rushed, moving the party along.

When my mother sat down at the table, she noticed the occasional black fly swirling around the food. They were common around town, the heat drawing them toward ripened fruit. Still, it was curious to see them in such a big house, landing on the white walls for all to see. A shiver ran down her spine as she remembered the black butterfly. Suddenly my mother wished she could be back with her nana María and el tío Kala in the little house by the funeral home. But her life was already turning in a new direction, one that would take her even farther away from her loved ones.

Before we moved to the United States, I met nana María briefly in her little house by the funeral home. Despite the fact that she was fighting cancer, she seemed strong. She was quick-witted, stunning those around her with her sturdy confidence. When she died from cancer a few months later, I watched people mourn her at the funeral home next door, as she'd seen so many others be mourned before it was her time. "When your nana left this world, she took secrets with her," Mom said. "We'll have to deal with the spirits on our own now that she's gone."

My brother was scared when my mom told us stories about nana María, but I always begged her for more details. When everyone fell asleep, I tried to picture my white-haired great-grandmother's kind face. But when I did, I never saw nana María's face; I visualized my own mother. I saw a woman of the North, born in the arid desert, strong, relentless, and magical. A woman willing to help me push away the demons and spirits.

7

EL CUARTITO

When I started fourth grade, the only thing that I craved was complete *silence*. At home in the trailer, my brother and I found ourselves ducking away from a constant stream of yelling and the clanking of pans. The house was full—five kids, including two toddlers, and four adults—and we all shared a small kitchen and one bathroom. The tighter you pack things, the more friction there is, the hotter it gets, and the easier it is for something to combust. Living in the trailer wasn't sustainable. That's physics.

The arguments escalated without any sign of abating. After years, my aunt was still disheveled and careless. My uncle drank more than I'd ever seen, going into drunken rages that were usually directed toward my aunt. The reality was that our families were growing. Fernando came first, plump and—as can be expected from a little brother—annoying. My cousin Andre followed a year after, twiggy and also annoying. There were babies everywhere, crying, screaming, losing their minds. Still, the friction between me and my brother and the petty fights we had with my cousins were minor. We were the appetizer, a limp salad served before the main course. The real action happened between my parents and of course between my uncle and aunt. The screaming, the throwing of random objects, the punches into the walls. I don't know how we evaded the attention of Kayla's grandparents, a sweet old white couple that lived next door. They must have been hard of hearing.

Sometimes I tried to visualize the paths of the yelling, like a bat using echolocation at night. I traced one argument from my dad and followed it to my uncle. It crisscrossed there and back, echoing through the thin walls before reaching my mom and my aunt and then bouncing back to my dad. Attempting to dampen the chaos was like undoing the cheap necklaces I begged my parents for at Claire's, a tedious and fruitless task. I tried to untangle the mess anyway.

The person that I had the hardest time untangling was my tío Miguel. When I was younger, I remember happy times with him. He had been a good uncle. But during the years that we spent living together with him and the rest of his family, I began to see into his deeper layers—erratic, angry, and illogical. He carried himself with an inflated sense of his own importance and walked with an arrogant swagger that annoyed me. It was as if wearing tucked-in Polo shirts somehow made him better than everyone else. Following the pattern my parents set, he enrolled his kids at Richardson. However, when Nurse Nelly suggested one day that my younger cousins might need to be tested for learning disabilities, Tío Miguel's machismo and elitism rose to the fore. He didn't admit or even acknowledge their delayed speech, lack of empathy, and inability to follow simple directions. The nurses suspected autism, perhaps ADHD. My mom and dad did as well. However, this narrative was one (of many) that my uncle was seemingly unable to accept. He behaved as if his kids had Camarillo blood, so they were fine, superior even. How dare *anyone* suggest otherwise?

Instead of receiving proper care, my cousins came face-to-face with my uncle's rage and punishment, suffering as he tried to force them into a mold they would never fit in. The oldest, Miguel Jr., whom we called Miguelito, sometimes had a hard time breathing and talking. He began to speak in a low voice, whispering with his head down as if in a constant state of fear. He'd hide under the table and play with toy cars, never outgrowing them—his back permanently hunched over. Andre was a little more lighthearted, a little less scared. He repeated words and phrases that he'd overhear, chirping like a parrot. Occasionally my brother and I would start the chain, saying something we knew he would cling to and repeat.

"Andre, close the door!" my brother sometimes yelled. Then we'd wait. Throughout the day, we'd hear Andre echo the same phrase from the room he shared with his parents at the back of the trailer. He'd walk to the fridge door and back. *Cierra la puerta, cierra la puerta, cierra la puerta.* Eventually we felt bad or grew annoyed and demanded, "Ya cállate, Andre, shut up!"

My dad would glance at us to show his disappointment. He'd gently pat Andre's curly hair—hair that my uncle refused to cut because it was almost blond, making him look more like a gringo—and tell him to come watch TV on the couch. My brother and I would stare with envy as he'd nudge Andre under his arm, gently reminding him that all the doors were already closed.

———————

The fight that changed everything had to do with *my* bedroom. The one with the green carpet, pink bed, and corner desk. *My* bedroom, the one where I did my homework and read the Bible, looking for mistakes and incongruities in the dense text. After dropping my brother and me off at school one day, Mom came back to the trailer to a scene she didn't expect. In the hallway, she heard screaming between my uncle and my aunt, which got louder when they saw my mom. Mom looked over to see what was going on and realized that my uncle was in my room, throwing my things through the open door. From the hallway, my mom yelled at him to stop.

"Are you mental?" she exclaimed, her lips tense. "Seriously, what the fuck is wrong with you people?"

"Cállate, pendeja!" my uncle yelled as he tore through my sheets and Barbies, their mangled bodies piling up on the already narrow hallway. We didn't have a cell phone; my mom had no way to dial for help inconspicuously. There was no point in calling the police, but she considered it, keeping the option open despite knowing there would be repercussions she didn't want to face. She could get my uncle deported, but then my dad's side of the family would turn on her even more.

Instead, she slowly paced backward toward the kitchen where the phone was, keeping her eyes on the entrance of my room in case my uncle started charging toward her as he had before. Pieces of my desk, keyboard, and hand-me-down Build-A-Bear collected on the floor, obstructing the way. She dialed hastily and quickly asked to speak with Edgar, my dad's name when he was at work. She waited for him to turn off his machine, wash the dust off his hands, wipe off his face, and walk over to the phone. She didn't wait for him to finish his sentence.

"Qué pasó—"

"Come home, Miguel has lost his shit."

Thirty minutes later, my dad arrived. That's when things got more heated. The source of my uncle's anger had to do with his opinion that I did not deserve my room. He needed more space; his boys needed more room. In some ways, I saw where he was coming from because I didn't actually sleep in there—I often slept next to my mom—but still, the room was *mine*. My dad paid for more of the trailer than my uncle did—often the entire month's rent. My uncle was unreliable and unpredictable. He drank often. Besides, the room was mine because I was the eldest of all the kids, I was the only girl, and because financially, I was entitled to it.

While my mom went off to pick my brother and me up from school, Dad stayed behind and got into it with my uncle, leaving both of them with bruised egos and regret. My dad wouldn't go into details. Deep down, I wondered if my dad felt like he'd lost his brother that day.

That night, as I tiptoed through my destroyed belongings, observing the mess that my uncle had made, a chill ran down my spine as it did when I walked through the blue shadows of the movie theater. My plywood desk was unusable. I put my old Barbies and stuffed animals in a bin and tossed the Bible in with the rest of the books. The pages were bent but they hadn't been torn. I didn't care for its contents either way. I was filled with a nauseating mix of guilt and anger. I felt unwanted in that room. I left things as they were and went into the comfort of my parents' room, where my mom had already laid my bed next to hers and turned on the TV to *Who Wants to Be a Millionaire*. The next day, we packed up our bags and left. My dad won the fight, but he lost the war. The trailer was under my uncle's name. There was nothing he could do about it.

———————

My mom had dreamed of leaving the trailer since the day we moved to Tucson. She wanted her own kitchen, her own place to fill up with stuff from discount racks and the classier items from TJ Maxx. She wanted to host friends. Over the years, Mom had taken me along to open houses on the other side of the river, asking about the rent and utilities. The houses she looked at weren't special—they were made of regular brick, and all had a sameness that I despised. All had similar driveways and were decorated in the same muted desert tones with the same plants against the same gravel backdrop. They weren't the glorious mid-century modern masterpieces or the western-style homes that people think of when they visualize life in Arizona. Instead, they had moldy wallpaper, dated shiplapped walls, and popcorn ceilings.

"It's a fixer-upper," Mom would say as she entered. "Nosotros podemos arreglarlo." When Dad would get home from work, Mom's eyes would brighten as she told him about the different houses. It wasn't long before my dad smashed her dreams: there was no option we could ever afford. They were all too expensive, requiring paperwork we couldn't fill out and down payments we couldn't make.

"Eliza, estan muy caras, please believe me—we can't afford that," my dad would say. "We can make it work," Mom would urge, her pleading falling on deaf ears. Instead, we ended up down the street, less than five minutes away from the trailer park, with mi tío Gabriel. My dad's youngest brother, Gabriel was somewhat of the rebel of the family. He shared traits with Dad and my uncle Miguel. He could be explosive and neurotic. He was often susceptible to conspiracy theories and didn't always believe the news. Still, he carried an air of confidence with him that Dad didn't. He drove through the streets of Tucson like they belonged to him. He demanded compensation when he got hit by another car. He wasn't afraid of the cops or ICE, even though he'd had close calls with both. Something about his confidence, his lack of regard for authority, and his innate rebelliousness seemed to protect him. He got away with things; he said *FUCK ICE*—loudly. He walked close to the edge while my dad shook his head and tensed his jaw on his behalf, carrying enough anxiety for the both of them.

Tío Gabriel told Dad that we could stay in the shed in the backyard as long as we needed, and since he was trying to pay off the property, we just had to help with rent. Nothing in the shed was up to code, but Tío Gabriel had installed plumbing and a bathroom. He'd laid the floor with off-white tiles from the Home Depot clearance section. Mom and Dad found a used bunk bed made out of black metal tubing, and my brother and I fought about which bunk we'd sleep in before my dad jumped in and assigned me the top bunk because I was taller.

Mom and Dad lined up the bunk bed next to their mattress, so that the bottom bunk was right by their heads. I looked down, wishing that I could switch with Fernando, as I thought of putting curtains down the side to create a little cave, or a cocoon of sorts. Instead, I watched my head and tucked myself in. Our first night there, I tried not to move. The metal pipes that held up the bed didn't feel secure, and they squeaked loudly when I turned. I lay awake worrying about the bed collapsing, thinking of my brother being crushed under my weight. Eventually I fell asleep to the sound of my family's steady breathing.

We called the glorified shed *el cuartito*. My dad told us— and assured Mom—that the little room was a temporary solution. Because it had no kitchen, before every meal my mom had to walk over a few steps to the trailer, where Uncle Gabriel lived with Aunt Denia, whom I loved for her patience and her level head. My teenage cousin Gabriel Jr.—who we all called Gabrielito—was there, too. He was my uncle's clone, except that he was organized, clean, and liked to keep his Nikes **white** in bold letters. It was easy for us to get along with my aunt and my cousin because there was enough space between us. El cuartito kept us isolated enough—happy and barely out of each other's hair.

The first few weeks, even months, living in el cuartito weren't all that bad. We'd all line up on my parents' bed in the shed to watch TV together, our body heat keeping one another warm. In the corner, my dad had managed to squeeze a dresser and a small desk for my computer. Somehow we managed to make what we needed fit, except for when we did laundry and our clothes would overflow out of stuffed drawers.

What took longer to get used to was how loud it was. We were right next to the train tracks, which were mere feet away behind the shed. Every so often, the vibration of a freight train going by would shake our already unstable beds and make the walls rattle. My mom often took my brother to the side of the tracks, tightly holding him and reminding him not to explore them alone. He'd wave at the train conductors, hoping that they would honk their horn as they passed by, squealing "El choo choo!" when they did. When Mom wasn't looking, Gabrielito and I would sneak out and place pennies on the tracks, letting the trains flatten them into oval blobs. Still, I avoided going there alone. Up close, the sheer size of the trains was startling—making you shake and feel insignificant as they passed by.

After a while, we stopped hearing the trains and noticing the rattling of our beds. Similar to the yelling, the sound of the trains became background noise.

———

After settling into el cuartito that summer, I started fourth grade. Later in the fall, my uncle showed up to the trailer with a puppy with a curled tail and a black snout. "We're going to call him Whiskey," my uncle declared—clearly proud of his creativity.

"You don't even drink whiskey," I teased. "Might as well call him Bud Light." I became obsessed with the dog. Whiskey was your typical orange mutt with short hair and lots of energy. We'd never been allowed to have a dog when we lived with my uncle

Miguel, but here at the new place with my uncle Gabriel, there was more space. From the day we got Whiskey, I tried to train him—spending hours in my uncle's backyard, which happened to face the playground at Laguna Elementary School. Now and again I found myself scanning the slides and swings, hoping one day I might see Kayla—our friendship was the one thing I missed about living in the trailer. Even if we were only minutes away, we were in different parks, no longer within the same borders. There were no more meet-ups at the swing set or stopping by each other's trailers to see if we could play. We might as well have been five hundred miles apart.

Whiskey made up for the loss of Kayla. He was the perfect dog—except that he liked to jump the fence. Time after time, the dog cops from the local ASPCA would try to catch him and put him in the pound. Every time he'd hop back into the yard and hide. Whiskey didn't need us to take him on walks—he was perfectly capable of doing that for himself. My mom and I found him endearing, taking him to the vet and feeding him boiled chicken, leftover Panda Express, and anything else that landed on our plates. The scraps were always his. When my mom went over the fence to cut nopales, an edible cactus she used for salads and smoothies, Whiskey would trail behind her, gliding over the fence effortlessly and trotting happily alongside her.

When I wasn't with Whiskey, I was focused on school. The week before Thanksgiving the following year, my fifth-grade teacher told us to draw our homes from an aerial perspective. It was supposed to be some sort of a bonding exercise that would make us feel grateful for what we had. For me, it was quite possibly the worst thing that could happen. By that point, I was over telling people that I was poor. I didn't want to draw attention to it. In some ways, I was starting to feel okay being lonely and concentrating more on school and less on chasing friendships. Instead, the gratitude exercise made me sick to my stomach as I began to outline the arrangement we had in el cuartito. I drew in where the beds were, side by side. I drew a square for the desk in the corner, another for the TV. I added an extra rectangle to show where the bathroom was and little slits to signal for windows. I shuddered when my teacher lingered over my shoulder, leaning in to see closer.

"Can you show me your work, Elizabeth?" she asked. I was hoping that she would glance quickly at my drawing and move on. It was basically a square with more squares, simple and insignificant. She lingered.

"This is where we live," I said, making sure to not specify *it* as home. "It's a guesthouse in my uncle's backyard. This is where my desk is." I pointed to the corner of the room, then trailed my finger over to the bunk beds my brother and I shared, the mini fridge, my parents' bed, and then the TV. My teacher was quiet, and I felt my face and neck grow hot with embarrassment. I wanted to shut down, but I panicked, wondering if I should have drawn a made-up house.

"It's only temporary; we'll be moving out soon," I hurriedly explained. I didn't tell her that the windows were lined with Styrofoam to help insulate the room. I didn't tell her that we had to share my uncle's kitchen or that I was afraid my bed would crush my brother or that when the train rumbled by, the whole place shook. I waited as she stared at the drawing.

"Good job, Elizabeth," she finally said, taking another indiscreet glance before moving on. I wondered what she thought of me, the same way I always wondered what my classmates thought of me. I watched her walk up and down the rows of desks, listening to everyone else describe their rooms and kitchens—their homes—colored in with their beautiful reality.

C omo te fue en la escuela?"
When I got home that day, Mom asked me what I did at school, as she always did.

"Pues, I had to draw where we live today," I said sheepishly as she sat me down and served me food. "Me dio pena," I continued. "I was embarrassed."

My mom's face went still, her lips pursed. I instantly regretted telling her, but she told me that she understood. When my dad got home from work a little while later, she told him about the assignment and that I'd drawn the room.

"Look at what your daughter has to do," she said, ashamed and regretful. "Are you proud of how we live?" My dad shook his head and started taking off his work clothes. He was covered in a thin layer of dust—corrosive specks filled with metallic particles that seeped deep into his skin.

"They've cut the amount of overtime I can take," he replied. "We can't afford more." From my bunk, I wondered if we'd live there forever, like parasites burrowing in somebody else's space, unable to survive without a host. Living in el cuartito wasn't temporary at all.

8

LA ESCONDIDA

The year 2008 hit us like a pile of bricks, but caught between my parents' work ethic and middle school, I barely noticed. My dad, who had always worked overtime, was suddenly at home more, his hours cut short. Although Fernando and I were entitled to food stamps, he didn't enroll us in the program, fearing the possible repercussions that any sort of welfare would have on his and my mom's ability to get papers. Because my brother and I were citizens, we would one day be able to start the residency process for our parents. Dad never lost hope in "one day," and my mom became obsessed with cutting coupons, ready to make a meal with whatever was on sale. Mexican women always make so much with so little. We never went hungry. And even though in other ways we might have needed more, we learned how to make do with less.

That year, we also added to our weekend routine, which otherwise included only church. On Saturday mornings while my dad was at work, Mom would drive Fernando and me to a nearby vacant lot where, on Friday nights, people drank and played loud music until the sun came up. On a good day, we'd find the ground littered with aluminum beer cans, all for the taking. Fernando and I would carefully avoid the cracked glass as we quickly helped Mom fill black trash bags with cans, sometimes flattening them with our feet to make more room. Over a span of a couple of weeks and multiple trips, we'd collect enough to sell at the scrapyard, a dirty metallic place that we weren't allowed to explore. While my parents dropped off the bags, Fernando and I stayed in the car listening to the sound of crushed metal fall onto itself.

Fer hated picking up cans for money. He hated how sticky and dirty the process felt. But I didn't complain. I liked that we could take trash and turn it into quick cash, and that in some ways, we were cleaning up and protecting that little bit of desert. When we got home to el cuartito, the thing I *did* complain about was not having good cable and the fun channels everyone else at school had. Even though I was no longer as desperate to be like—and liked by—the popular girls at school, I still wanted to watch what all the other kids watched. I wanted to be able to chime into conversations about the newest episode of *Hannah Montana* or *SpongeBob*. I wanted to feel like I belonged. Instead, I was stuck with a steady stream of the news, the Spanish channel, and reruns of the same public broadcasting shows—all of it reminding me that I didn't fit in, that I was different, that even though I was American, I couldn't relate to American pop culture because I didn't have access to it.

But every time I grumbled about money, making some comment to my parents about our not having enough, my dad reminded me of the beach property we had in Mexico.

"Mija, you have so much more than everyone else, remember that," he assured me, his eyes widening. "La Escondida is yours." La Escondida was the thing that he fell back on when things were going to shit or when we truly *felt* poor. La Escondida was our lottery ticket, our pot of gold at the end of the rainbow. It was a fantasy we hoped would one day make us rich.

My dad bought La Escondida for a good price in 1999, right before we moved to Tucson. He'd heard stories about the untouched land next to Sonora's virgin beaches from my grandfather and Tío Miguel, who frequented the area while buying fresh seafood that he could resell to restaurants in Arizona.

"We should go see what's out there," Dad told my mom. "Maybe we can buy ourselves a little plot of land and build a house by the ocean." There my parents met a rancher named Jesús. Don Jesús lived humbly, calling the land he lived on La Escondida, the Hidden Place.

"Would you ever be open to selling a lot of land?" my dad asked.

"Mijo, I'm old. I'm happy to sell it all," Don Jesús replied with a smile, glancing out toward the horizon. "Go see the view from the dunes before you make up your mind. It's a beautiful view wherever you look."

Most of my early memories of La Escondida are from the back of a moving truck, my hands tightly holding on to its sides as I try not to fall off at every sharp turn. My cousins Ana Claudia and Martín and I would always beg to ride in the back of the truck, our scrawny legs extended into the plastic cargo bed, our bodies light and the sand in the air tickling our skin. We lived for the adrenaline rush of the car speeding through the desert as we pointed out the snakes and rabbits hiding among the dense areas filled with prickly chollas.

Eventually we'd make it to the bottom of a hill that led up to the dunes, where my dad would park the truck. If he went any farther it would get stuck in the sand, even if he had four-wheel drive on. My cousins and I would put on our sandals, topple out the back, and run through the dunes ahead of everyone. As we ran, our feet sank into the dunes, the hot grainy sand finding its way between our toes. My cousin Martín would go off into the bushes to pee while we trekked ahead, calling back: "Hurry up, Martín, we're going to beat you!"

When we finally got close to shore, we saw something we'd never seen before: a whale, or rather, what was left of one. Its large ribs, bleached and white, extended into the air, pointing at the clouds. Ana Claudia hovered around it, rolling pieces of scattered vertebrae in the sand, each the size of a tree stump. While our parents caught up, my cousins and I climbed on its ribs, our small hands clinging to the curved structure. To us, the whale skeleton looked like a ship to another world. We repurposed the carcass, making it our playground by the sea. The whale had once been a majestic being, gliding its way through the ocean, but we didn't think about that. We didn't think about its life or its death. We didn't question why it had ended up here on the beach, alone and rotting. We weren't yet afraid of death.

———

La Escondida increased in value over the years in the way that land usually does. It was a beachfront property close to the beaches in Rocky Point, which was easy for American tourists to access. In the desert, any property with freshwater sources is valuable. La Escondida, with its three natural wells and two unobstructed kilometers of beachfront, was a gold mine. You didn't have to be a developer—any person with an ounce of vision could see its financial potential. A few miles north, private hotels were being built on plots of land similar to ours, marketed to tourists as an "oasis in the desert." But La Escondida became a complicated piece of land for our family, one that would follow us wherever we went.

In the months leading up to 2006, an American named Rob Carnivale began to make calls to my father, telling him to vacate the land. At first the threats sounded like a scam, one of many pulled off by extortionists in Mexico trying to get a quick buck. As the calls continued, my dad became cautious, paranoid even, suspecting that he was being watched. On his trips to Mexico to sell used cars, he received messages from people related to Carnivale, asking to see him in person. Concerned for his safety, he refused. By then, he knew that Carnivale was a real person and the owner of the land next door to La Escondida. His land was called Santo Tómas, an area that was marketed as a private and secure beach community off the beaten path. It seemed clear that Carnivale was the type of person willing to hurt people to get ahead.

In 2006, my dad received a court notice from Carnivale and his legal team. Carnivale claimed to have documentation proving that our land was his, demanding that my father hand over his paperwork to him, the rightful landowner. We all knew it was bullshit. At home, my dad would spend day and night ranting.

"Rob Carnivale es un pendejo, a rat," he said after getting

updates from my grandfather. "Tengo que mandarles dinero, I have to send my parents money for legal fees," he told my mom, shaking his head. Mom was frustrated, transfixed on our own expenses and our lack of space.

"But you just sent them money, Rubén. We need it here," she stammered.

Angrily Dad replied, "If you want to be in charge of our finances, do it yourself, but if we lose La Escondida, we'll have nothing left." Sometimes I would interject myself into their argument.

"No puedes convertir la arena en dinero," I said. "You can't turn sand in Mexico into money in America." He would insist that I wait; that I hold on to the hope of "one day." He told me to believe in him.

Little by little, our savings shrank. By the time the financial crisis hit in 2008, my grandfather had asked my dad to sign over a piece of La Escondida to him as payment. Without any other choice, he did, only to find out soon after that my grandfather had then signed it over to his brothers, el tío Miguel and el tío Alfredo. When this happened, my mom erupted.

"Why would you give *them* anything?" she argued. "All they've done their whole life is take what doesn't belong to them." Mom wasn't wrong—we all knew it.

"It's not like I had a choice. I gave the land to my father. What he does with it is up to him," Dad said. "What am I supposed to do, lose La Escondida for another petty fight? I have to pay my dad." And so, through a legally binding document, my dad's brothers profited once more from the dysfunction.

I never understood why Abuelo Marcelino would charge his

own son for his services, especially when he knew of our financial situation and had seen the way we lived in el cuartito. But like most things, I downplayed it, chalking it up to typical family dynamics. It was painful to think badly of my grandfather, someone I'd always admired and respected. It was too hard to think of someone so knowledgeable making mistakes. I could never imagine my own father doing something like that to me. But I wouldn't let myself think too much about it. Besides, I was preoccupied with school and my newfound obsession with MySpace and YouTube.

The internet opened my world up, giving me the access that I so desperately craved to information and faraway places. I didn't need religion or my parents to help me answer difficult questions. I was no longer limited by Spanish TV or whatever was playing on Univision. With the click of a button, I could tap into the endless stream of knowledge at my fingertips to help me make something of myself. So while my parents fought about money, I learned how to torrent music illegally, filling my Walkman with songs by Eminem and Kelly Clarkson, balancing my rage and my inability to process my emotions. Through my obscure CD mixes, I gave myself some form of therapy, blocking out the fighting in our glorified shed—my headphones becoming the only walls between us. I no longer needed the promise of some distant piece of land. I no longer needed to pin my hopes on the mirage of La Escondida. Instead, I could pin my hopes on something closer and more solid. I could pin my hopes on myself.

9

HOLY WARS

By the end of our years of middle school, everyone had Motorola Razr flip phones, which made it easy for my classmates to plan weed breaks in the girls' bathrooms and to flirt with boys soaked in Axe body spray. I didn't have a phone or a boy to flirt with. I got nothing but more body hair and homework, enough of both to drain me of the need to experience the things most of my classmates were. As it always had, school continued to be a driving and distracting force in my life: driving me to succeed, to be the best inside the classroom, and distracting me from everything outside of it—from the drama in the hallways to the yelling in el cuartito. School was my ticket to a future I couldn't see, but devoutly believed in. But in eighth grade, as I inched closer to high school years—the years that *really* mattered for college admissions—the protective walls of the classroom began to crack, and it became impossible to ignore the growing anti-immigrant environment in Arizona and everything that was at stake because of it.

On April 23, 2010, Governor Jan Brewer signed the Support Our Law Enforcement and Safe Neighborhoods Act into law. Better known as SB 1070 or the "show me your papers" law, it allowed police officers to ask anyone, at any time, to show their immigration papers to prove that they were here legally. Police could arrest anyone, even without a warrant, if they even *suspected* the person was here without papers. And if you didn't have your papers on you when asked, you could be charged with a misdemeanor and face prison time. The law encouraged racial profiling and harassment, while violating constitutional and civil rights.

Across Tucson, the fear was palpable. People stopped driving, not wanting to leave their houses because they could be stopped not for committing a heinous crime, but for looking a certain way, speaking a certain way. They could be stopped based on a police officer's "discretion"—their suspicion, perception, wariness. And if U.S. history has taught us anything, a police officer's "discretion" is often rooted in racism, whether their own or that of the racist institution signing their checks.

As the air grew thick with heat and anxiety, the whisper networks got busier.

"Don't go into work today."

"Avoid the supermarket in South Tucson for the next few days."

"Don't answer questions, you have the right to remain silent."

Even Mexican radio stations warned us of raids. "Nos han alertado de ruedadas cerca de la Grant Road," they'd say. "Around a hundred migrants have been taken into custody." When these announcements happened, we stayed quiet, listening intently.

My parents were here on valid tourist visas, which allowed them to enter the country legally for vacation, to visit friends and family, to shop. But the tourist visa was clear about one thing: your *visit* was temporary. While the tourist visa might be valid anywhere from a month to ten years after it's been issued, you can stay in the United States for only a maximum of 180 days each entry. Intending to stay permanently on a tourist visa is considered committing visa fraud. So while tourist visas may not have offered my parents much shelter, as a family we felt we had a thin layer of protection because we knew our way around the rules. We had our scripts of what to say and what not to say if we were questioned; we knew what to wear and what not to wear. We knew how to play the part.

SB 1070 stripped us of what little protection we had felt. While my parents had always told me that my citizenship meant that I could go to a police officer if I needed help, it was different now. How do you protect yourself from discretion? How do you not look the part when the part is stripped of its nuance and reduced to merely being Brown skinned? When I left for school in the mornings, I began to fear that my parents wouldn't be there when I got back home. Despite the fact that we lived here illegally on tourist visas, the only other time I had feared being separated from my parents was when I was learning about heaven in catechism at St. Elizabeth Ann Seton Catholic Church on Sundays.

My mom had put me into catechism when I was young, insisting I have all my holy sacraments. Grudgingly I'd gone through it and eventually made a trip to Mexico so that I could have my first communion at the local church in Caborca. By the time that Fernando turned six, he was stuck in Sunday school with me, where they tried brainwashing him with cartoon drawings of Jesus on the cross. What made this whole experience worse was the fact that Dad didn't even believe in God.

"This is going to make them believe in nonsense," he said to my mom. "They don't really need to waste their time on this." Still, Mom was adamant.

"They can make up their own mind when they're older," she replied. "Besides, it's a good thing for them to do." It's not like my mother was a devout Catholic, but she had faith. She'd say, "Gracias a dios," after something good happened. But I came from a family of atheists—or rather, atheist men. Mi abuelo Marcelino would assure me, even as a young child, that there was no god, while my mother would tell me about Noah's saving all the animals on his ark, as well as stories of diosito and his plight to save us all. I would nod my head, unsure of what the truth was, as my mother's stories clashed with my dad's and my grandfather's words in my head.

At church, people told me that I had a holy name, the name of a saint. I wondered if saints despised catechism as much as I did. I just had weekends off from school and I had to spend one of those days in church. Maybe I'd have been more eager to give up one of my free days if catechism was fun or interesting or even just not soul-crushingly boring. We listened to lessons on doctrines and repeated prayers in Spanish because despite the fact that I spoke English fluently, my parents enrolled me in Spanish catechism with the other Mexicans. We got a half-hour break, during which we'd eat snacks and complain to one another in English, wondering why church had to be such a drag. After class, the catechism teachers stood by the entrance to mass, counting us off one by one to check that we were attending; to make sure we were on our way toward some sort of eternal salvation.

At first I waited for catechism to become more interesting, as happened with subjects at school. But as time went on, I grew annoyed and confused by the inconsistencies between what I knew was fact and what the teacher, Mr. Pablo, told us. "The earth was formed in only six days," he said poetically.

Eyebrows raised, I would throw in: "That doesn't explain evolution, Mr. Pablo." I watched Mr. Pablo's composed face contort. From the way he dressed and spoke, I figured Mr. Pablo thought that he was better than most people. As if reading a little book could somehow elevate him above sinners like me.

"Those without faith will be lost," he replied, eagerly trying to move on.

"What will happen to those without faith?" I pried. "Are they not also God's children?"

"They will not find heaven, Elizabeth," he said. "That's why we must have faith, why we must not sin." Unsatisfied, I listened to Mr. Pablo explain the effects of sin. "Sins stain you like grime to a sponge. If one sins too much, the stain becomes permanent."

After class, I thought about my grandfather and my father. I thought about their lack of faith. They believed in the big bang and science and in the idea that death is final. For a long time, I pictured heaven to be a place full of the people one loves. At that moment, I made up my mind. I decided that I didn't want to go to a heaven where the faithless will not be welcome; I decided that a heaven without my father and grandfather would be something closer to hell.

For years I played the part in catechism, eventually being picked to speak in front of the congregation. I hated doing it—mostly because they made me wear a black robe over my cute-ass outfits—but Mom forced me to. I'd get up in front of a mass, in a room full of people who were faithful or pretended to be, and I'd address the crowd, reading the sermon in perfect Spanish.

Afterwards, strangers would come up to my parents, telling them: "Your daughter is an angel." Old people love kids who have faith. I watched my parents gleam with pride—even my dad showed off his rare perfect smile. I'd nod my head at the praise and thank them while wondering if they really believed the words that I said onstage. Ultimately, I felt relieved that they couldn't tell that I didn't.

In eighth grade—my final year of catechism—as the anti-immigrant laws were introduced and gained nationwide attention, my church teacher Mr. Pablo asked us all to think about something that we would give up for lent. The other students came up with everything from video games to chocolate. I picked Flamin' Hot Cheetos.

That same day, my dad picked me up from catechism and none of us felt like going to mass, not even my mom. My dad and I headed up toward Mr. Pablo, who was waiting to count the students attending mass. We checked in with him and smiled. When he wasn't looking, we snuck away and headed to the car. On the way back to my uncle's backyard, to the glorified shed we called home, I asked my dad to stop at the Quik Mart. He did, grabbing himself a soda, while I bought a bag of Flamin' Hot

Cheetos and enjoyed the crackle of each crunch as we headed home. It seemed to me that the institution of religion was as fickle and divisive as the institution that enacts anti-immigration laws, both separating families on earth as it is in heaven.

10

FOOL'S GOLD

There have been lots of things that pointed to: okay, immigrants are not welcome here. You're welcome to come here and work and do all the dirty work. You're welcome here to come and work the fields. You're welcome to come and work the hotels. You're welcome to come and cut the grass, and watch my kids, and do the laundry. But you're not welcome to be a human being here. That was the message immigrants had.

—Petra Falcon,
Executive Director of Promise Arizona (PAZ)

By the time that I was a freshman in high school, the younger generation—my generation—got louder, in contrast to the whisper networks of our elders. The day before Governor Brewer signed SB 1070 into law, teenagers from high schools across Tucson traveled to Phoenix to fill the streets and march together to the capitol building in protest. College students with signs gathered outside as the bill was inked. Government officials were expecting the law to scare us into silence and flight but failed to consider our anger, as our parents were herded, detained, and barred from basic human rights.

In 2010, only a month after SB 1070 was signed—which made it legal to racially profile and arrest us—lawmakers came for us again with the passing of HB 2281, a bill that restricted us from learning about our culture in the classroom by banning ethnic studies from K–12 public schools. Award-winning books by Mexican American authors were banned and a Mexican American studies program that had flourished in Tucson for more than a decade was disbanded. The state threatened to withhold funding for districts that didn't comply.

The youth refused to comply. I watched social media become our generation's whisper network, making it possible for people like me to connect and organize. Through walkouts and demonstrations, national attention was brought to Arizona in support of immigrants. I still remember the contrast between our public actions and outward resistance and our inner fear and exhaustion. All of us lived in the tension of duality.

Despite always encouraging me to stand up to authority—to know that my citizenship protects me—my parents wouldn't let me participate in the protests.

"No te atrevas," my dad directed.

"Stay out of it," my mom concurred. Over the years, my parents had seen activists and journalists silenced in Arizona. They figured it was only a matter of time for the same to happen to citizens speaking out.

"If you get arrested, if anything happens, you'll be stained forever," Dad said. "It would ruin your future." No shock here: my education still took priority for them, and missing school was not an option. I had to care about my education even if my education didn't care about my culture.

On top of that, my parents' situation as immigrants in the United States had become direr. Their tourist visas were set to expire a few months later, on January 11, 2011. At that point, they'd have to reapply for visas. Though they'd gone through the process before, it hadn't been in an environment as strained and anti-immigrant as the one we were now in.

"But why am I supposed to stand around when people are getting treated this way?" I asked my dad one day in el cuartito.

"Tune out the noise," he instructed. "Ponte las pilas." My first semester of high school was spent with my nose in my books, focused on doing what I did best: being the best student. Online, I stumbled upon blogs on college admissions and found my way into forums where students shared resources and insider information on what it took to get into the top universities in the country. Harvard, Yale, Columbia—all places featuring ivy-covered bricks and an air of secrecy. The more I learned about these schools, the more I began to wonder if they were even real places. Were they just another fantasy or were they something that I could make a reality? I switched out of fun, unweighted electives like photography, fashion, and choir and into ones that would impress an admissions counselor. Little by little, I felt myself becoming an image of someone else. An image that required me to shed bits and pieces of my personality.

I had my education under control, and as my parents weighed the risks of staying in the United States on expired tourist visas or going back to Mexico to reapply for a new one, they assured me that they had *their* situation under control. I trusted them. Or maybe I simply wasn't capable of not trusting them, of thinking about what either option could mean. My little brother, barely in second grade, certainly didn't understand. The truth was that it was common for people like my parents to stay in the United States after their tourist visas expired. But that month, with the anti-immigrant fervor in Arizona beating down on us as hard as the desert sun, my parents made the difficult decision to go back to Mexico and reapply for a new tourist visa.

"It's better this way," they explained to me. "With a tourist visa, being in the United States isn't illegal, only working is." In a way, they reduced the total amount of punishment they were willing to take in exchange for Fernando and me to have an opportunity in America.

"Legally, we'd be better off with some sort of visa in hand," Dad continued. My brother cried when my mom explained to him that they'd have to leave for Mexico soon.

"This is a process we have to do across the border, Fer," she cooed. "We'll be back before you know it." I heard her repeat something I'd heard my whole childhood. "It's only temporary."

My parents' verbal reassurances were in stark contrast to what I witnessed. Little by little, I watched them fight more as the stress of their deadline loomed. My dad and my tío Gabriel weren't really on speaking terms by then, either, after a petty argument they'd had over the truck my dad took to work. This, combined with the stress of having to leave us behind for a bit, led to us leaving el cuartito a month before my parents were scheduled to head to Mexico. We'd be moving in with my mom's friend Rosario.

"It's easier for us all to be here together right now," Mom

explained. "And you'll stay at Rosario's house while we're gone."

As my world began to crumble around me, I gripped on to the things that I found constant. My English teacher required us to do the same type of essay every week. My math teacher always gave us quizzes on Tuesdays. As January 11 approached, my parents stayed busy working and finalizing logistics, while I found ways to distract my little brother and make sure he stayed on top of his schoolwork.

Three days before my parents were set to leave, on their anniversary, there was a mass shooting at one of the local Safeways, where Gabby Giffords, one of the only progressive members in the U.S. House of Representatives of Arizona, had been speaking at a local event. A gunman had shot Giffords in the head and then fired into the crowd.

"A little girl that goes to our church was hit," Mom told us that evening. "She didn't make it." Selfishly, I was relieved when I found out that the shooter was white. I was tired of watching immigrants become scapegoats while the real threats to safety were ignored. It had always felt like the real threat to safety was never looked at, never examined. I guess white skin and guns weren't considered to be a suitable combination to villainize.

––––––––

A few days after the shooting, I watched my parents mechanically pack their bags with the essentials and nothing more, load them into the car, and drive away. I waved at them as they left, one hand in the air and the other squeezing my brother's shoulder as he cried. My dad waved back before making a turn down the driveway. I saw my mom in the passenger side with a faintly sad smile. When their car disappeared from view, I swallowed down my own feelings, trying not to become preoccupied with the emptiness that I felt. Back in the house, Rosario helped me set up the tubed metal bunk beds we'd had in el cuartito. Now they'd be in the room Fer and I shared with her two young kids, Carlos and Lupito, who were seven and four respectively. As the oldest, I tried to maintain some order, checking to be sure that all the boys made their beds and cleaned up after themselves. I wanted to help Rosario out as much as possible as well as maintain my own sanity.

"I'm never having kids," I'd murmur to myself as they wreaked havoc in the small space we were forced to share.

After a couple of weeks, I stopped keeping track of how long my parents had been away. I was getting back into the routine of schoolwork, soccer practice, and babysitting the boys. My downtime—the little I had—was spent helping Fer out with his homework and researching how to shape myself into the ideal college applicant. Outside of the occasional joke to my friends about being an orphan while my parents were in Mexico, I said nothing about my family's situation.

Two months into our stay with Rosario, she came into the bedroom we all shared and handed me the phone. From the top of my bunk, I got the news I never wanted.

"Elizabeth, nos la negaron otra vez," I heard my mom whisper. "We're not going to be able to come back."

Their tourist visa application had been denied. *Twice.* I was in shock. My parents had paid lawyers, spent tons of money, and gone to the U.S. embassy in Mexico, padfolios filled with documents. Along with the visa application, they had to prove that they lived in Mexico through phone bills, taxes paid, and who knows what else, while also proving that they were deserving of visiting the United States. After all my parents' documents, applications, and forms on forms, the U.S. agents got to use their damn *discretion* to decide if they wanted to approve it or not. When my parents were denied the first time, they were given no reason as to why. So they did what they were supposed to: they reworked their case, paid more money, filled out more paperwork, and went back to see if they had a second chance.

Denied again.

With no explanation, again.

Maybe the agents knew they'd been living in the United States. Maybe they suspected that they would come over the border to work—after all, they were. Maybe my dad was nervous, and they could see him sweating through his black shirt. The agent told them not to apply again for at least three years.

It was worded as a suggestion, but my parents knew what it meant. They'd been banned, blacklisted. They were somewhere in a database full of names: people with hopes and dreams; people with families, children with U.S. citizenship; people naive enough to believe in the American dream, naive enough to believe they were worthy of it.

My tears thawed my frozen state of disbelief, and I began to sob as I handed the phone to my little brother. Before he even held it up to his ear, I watched the tears well up on his small face. I threw myself down on the top bed, quickly hiding my face in my pillow and trying to calm down so as to not further scare Fernando.

I wondered if the pain I felt would kill me. I wondered if the fact that my breathing hurt was a sign of my body's giving up. As quietly as I could, I gasped for air, listening to my brother scream and cry for our mother from the bunk below. Eventually I crawled down the ladder, picked up his small eight-year-old body, and cradled him, gently massaging his head as he held back his own tears.

"I'll keep you safe, Fer," I told him. "I won't ever abandon you." After a while, we both fell asleep, unsure of what the next day would bring.

———————

My brother's eyes were swollen the next day, but he had calmed down. As if nothing had happened, I got him ready for school, gathering our things and making sure his home-work was neatly placed in his color-coded folders. After dropping him off, I headed to the bus stop, where I waited for my ride to school. During math class, Mr. Becker announced that tran-scripts with our first-semester grades were out. I watched students get up in line as he printed them out for us. I stayed seated, listen-ing to people howl and hoot at barely passing grades. "Close call," they'd say, exhaling a sigh of relief.

Eventually Mr. Becker came over to me, noticing how quiet I'd been. "Look at the number on the bottom of the page," he said as he handed it over to me.

Straight As, a 4.0 GPA. And a ranking that told me that I was first in my class.

"You should be proud of yourself," he said, smiling and giv-ing me a pat on the shoulder. I stared at the number, numb to what it might mean. Instead I thought about how easily I could lose my footing, how easily I could lose that ranking. I hadn't told anyone about my parents' visa applications being denied, but deep in my gut I knew that I had to keep going. I felt myself get angry and hot, frustrated by the unfairness of it all. But then my mind did what it had always done: went back to working on solutions. I'd have to mobilize. I knew that the only chance I would have to be in the United States long-term was if I came up with a plan for *exactly* how I would stay and survive without my parents. I knew that they would have concerns; I knew I had concerns. But more than that, I knew that I could be separated from my parents, but I refused to be separated from my education, from the future I couldn't see but devoutly believed in.

11

PATHS THE CLOUDS TAKE

During the period we were separated from our parents, I would take Fer to the park almost every day. Most times I'd bring a textbook and homework that I could do while he played. But every so often I would leave the house empty-handed, subconsciously allowing myself to be the fifteen-year-old kid I was and not the exhausted middle-aged mom that I had come to feel like over the past two months. My memories of that time are hazy, due to the pressure I was under, but one afternoon is seared into my mind, one I will never forget.

Fer and I sat beside each other in the park, our legs cooled by the grass and our necks craned upward toward the sky. He had been learning about clouds in his second-grade class at Richardson Elementary.

"That one is a cumulus, and those over there are cirrus," he explained in his squeaky little voice. I knew nothing about clouds, so I took his word for it. We watched them drift and morph and even disappear as he used his vibrant imagination to color his newly acquired knowledge, pointing out a stratocumulus cloud that looked like a spaceship.

"Clouds can't pick what they are, they just *are*," he continued. "They have to go where the wind takes them."

I was impressed by everything he knew about clouds, even if he was unaware of the wisdom he'd dropped, the parallels to his life. While the clouds didn't fascinate me as much as they did Fer, I was struck by his ability to learn, to retain all this information. It felt so grown-up. He was still such a baby in my eyes, but I was beginning to see how quickly he was growing up. I wondered what he would remember about this time in his life, about this situation we were in.

Would he remember the unpredictability of it all? Would he look back and feel abandoned by our parents? Would he remember these clouds on this day the same way I would? Would he remember doing our homework together on Rosario's kitchen table? Would he remember our misfit bunk beds that miraculously never collapsed? Would he look back and feel as much pressure as I did?

We continued to search the sky for new shapes and formations, but I was admittedly distracted by considering what he might remember and what would become of him in the future. Where would the wind take him? I knew I wanted to stay in the United States—I *had* to stay in the United States—but what we had was not sustainable. I could not continue to grind my way into being the best student, the one who needed to remain ranked number one and still play sports and join a student club. I probably had to start a new club, too, after reading that colleges really like when students show initiative and investment. I could not fill out my future college applications with honors and volunteer hours if I also had to play parent to my eight-year-old brother.

But what about *his* future? His education? I felt my heart start to beat faster, reality weighing heavy on me as anxiety pumped through my body. While my parents and I hadn't ever directly talked about it, in my mind I thought that Fer would be with me for a few more months, until the end of the school year. But then what? It was impossible to plan a future when you were trying to survive in the present.

"That cirrus cloud looks like a feather!" His wandering thoughts brought me and my very tethered thoughts back to the park. To the clouds. To the two of us—brother and sister—being kids.

"It *does* look like a feather!" I told him, trying to match his enthusiasm and mask my unease. Before I finished the sentence, the feather began to disperse, and within seconds, the cloud disappeared.

One afternoon the following week I got back to Rosario's house after school and Fer wasn't there. At first, I figured he was in the bathroom or in the backyard. Maybe he'd decided to run off with his friends at the park by the school to watch clouds. As I set my backpack on the kitchen table, Rosario walked in with the same guilty, sad face she'd had when she handed me the phone and my parents told me their visas had been denied. I felt my chest tighten as fear trickled down my spine and all I could think was, *He is my responsibility.* Sure, we had Rosario, but if Fer was upset, he came to me. If it was bedtime, I was getting him ready. I was the one ensuring his schoolwork was done, that he was eating enough, and I was the one trying to protect him from everything going on. With our parents in Mexico, Fer and I clung to each other as the only nuclear family we had.

"Is my brother okay?" I asked Rosario.

"You should call your parents," she replied.

It was my dad who answered the phone. "Cómo estás, mija?" he said. I felt my face burn hot.

"Fer isn't home. Where is he!" I shouted.

"He is okay, don't worry. It's okay." He tried to calm me down. "Your uncle Alfredo picked him up from school earlier today and brought him here." He paused. "He is with us."

His words blurred together as my breath quickened. I listened to him dodge my questions and grew angry by the ease in his voice. "Sabía que te ibas a enojar. I knew you'd argue," he said, as if my feistiness was to blame for the harshness of his decision, as if they didn't teach me to stand up to authority when I knew I was being wronged. "Está muy chiquito, he was too little to stay there without us." He kept talking, but I didn't register what he said because of the red that I was seeing.

First, some random U.S. official carelessly decided my parents couldn't be in the country, that they weren't worthy of even visiting the States, let alone working jobs no one else wanted and living here with their children. But now? Now my parents had callously decided that Fer couldn't be here with me, that I was not even worthy of a heads-up, let alone getting to say goodbye. The situations were different, but the betrayal felt the same.

My rage turned to tears until it felt like I didn't have any left to cry. Or at least until I realized that I had homework I needed to finish before school tomorrow. I began to wonder if I needed my education more for the future it would provide or because it was so good at distracting me from the present.

I woke up the next morning to the jarring emptiness of Fer's lower bunk—the bunk I had always wanted. There was a slower pace to my morning routine because I just had to get myself ready for school. I trudged through the school day on autopilot, and as soon as I got out of class, I headed to Richardson. The teachers there had often felt like an extended family, and I needed that familiar and familial connection now more than ever.

After school over the next several weeks, I sought solace in Fer's old classroom. Miss Almodoba let me come whenever I wanted. She told me that all the little second graders asked where Fer was, insisting that she leave his desk exactly where it was with his name tag still on it, and the jacket he left still on the chair. They wanted everything to be there for when he came back. Fer's class was so united. He fit in with other kids in a way that I never did, and I hated that he had to be ripped away from them.

I wondered what the best way was to tell eight-year-olds that Fer wasn't coming back. I wondered if my parents had even told *Fer* that he wasn't coming back. I wondered if I would ever go back to Mexico or if the last couple of months of my freshman year in high school would be it for me in the United States. After Fer was taken away from me, I lost a bit of the will I had to mobilize, to plan for how I would stay—not to mention also losing some of the certainty to know if staying would really be worth it. Was choosing education over my family really the right choice? Or by choosing my education was I also choosing my family?

One afternoon I was venting to Miss Almodoba, who had

basically become my therapist, telling her how fucked up the whole situation was and how there was still a part of me that wanted to stay, how I was keeping my grades up during all of this, and how I still had plans for college here. But I also confessed that I didn't know if I had the same drive anymore and I questioned if any of it was worth it.

Her classroom door opened and the computer lab teacher, Mrs. Hernandez—the same one I had for four years when I was at Richardson—walked in. After hearing the long story made short, Mrs. Hernandez quickly—and seemingly way too easily—said, "If you need somewhere to stay to finish high school, you can stay with me and my family."

Shocked, I looked at Miss Almodoba, who added, "I also know someone who could help with the process. Merva, the mother of one of my students, has a mom on the school board and has helped tons of kids in tough situations. I bet they would be willing to help you figure out what you have to do so you can stay at the Hernandezes'."

I felt my shoulders relax as a tentative hopeful smile lit up my face. The visceral reaction proved what I already knew deep down: I had always wanted to stay. I *needed* to stay. I had simply started to feel like it was impossible, fearing that I wouldn't have anyone to stay with—especially after realizing that Rosario had too much on her plate to let me stay long term. It wasn't so much that I lost my desire or drive, it was more that I was trying to brace myself for the inevitable disappointment that comes when your parents don't have the right papers; when you're a first-generation Mexican American.

I still had doubts that Mrs. Hernandez would really let me

stay with her and her family when it came down to it. Her offer was so nonchalant that it almost felt like one of those moments where you see someone you haven't seen in a long time and you both say you should make plans to hang out and catch up, knowing damn well you aren't going to. Still, I felt hopeful and cautiously confident that even if my offer to stay at Mrs. Hernandez's house fell through at the last minute, the offer itself was still the first step. The second step, and arguably the biggest one, was that I had to convince my parents to let me.

For the remainder of my freshman year, I kept the plan from them. I knew it would be better to talk in person when I went to Mexico for the summer. I rushed off phone calls with them, blaming sports practice or homework, because I didn't trust myself to not say anything. I was eager to get their permission, but I knew I had to be strategic. I was not a cloud, like Fer, having to go wherever the wind would take me. I was too stubborn to surrender my control in that way. Instead, I would harness the power of the wind and use it to help me complete what I set out to do.

I ended the school year still ranked number one in my class. And despite knowing differently, I left Fer's lower bunk empty the entire time, like the second graders left his desk, so that it would be there for him when he came back.

12

BIENVENIDOS A MÉXICO

With Fer gone, I spent hours lying awake in his bunk while Rosario's kids snored next to me. My mind drifted back to the memories I had from before my parents had their visas denied, back when we were able to drive to Mexico for the holidays and short summer trips. My brother and I always looked forward to our visits, happy to have the chance to see our grandparents and cousins, eager to walk across the street for Popsicles and ice-cold Mexican Coca-Cola. Everything in Mexico tasted different, filled with richness. The Coke was made with real sugar, and nothing was more refreshing than when the coldness of the glass bottle hit my lips on those sweltering summer days. My dad would always say that he would rather buy me a soda than get one for himself because he loved seeing me so happy. I wanted him to enjoy the sweetness of life, too, so I found myself buying him one with spare change I'd saved. That way, we could enjoy it together.

Maybe that's why everything in Mexico tasted sweeter and familiar—we were together. Being there gave us a freedom we didn't have in the United States. My brother and I could run to the plaza by ourselves or be lazy huevones all day, endlessly flipping through the TV channels and watching cartoons and movies in Spanish. Without the stress and fear of persecution, of looking behind our backs for ICE, the police, or border patrol, we rested. In Mexico, nobody could tell us to leave. In Mexico, we were home.

On those trips, crossing into Mexico was seamless. Once we reached the border city of Nogales, which had both a Mexican and an American side, Mexican border agents would let us pass through without questioning where we came from or who we were. My dad would nod at them, almost as if saying *What's up?,* and they'd smile and wave as we crossed over to the other side, back in our land. From that point, the countryside changed drastically. Instead of the boring uniform yards and comfortable houses on the American side, people in Nogales decorated their homes with bright pinks, greens, and purples. The yard art was eclectic and made out of metal—some pieces showing more wear than others, all somehow still standing upright.

As we passed through in our car, we were greeted by merchants and street vendors, many preparing to cross over to the United States by foot. My mom always rolled down her window and handed them whatever change had gathered in the cup holders as she wished them good luck. In Mexico, it even smelled different, sometimes appetizing like fresh conchas right out of the oven, sometimes nauseating like gasoline. We'd pass large semis transporting merchandise, weaving through the chaos as my stomach churned. We all got carsick from the industrial smog that was emitted within and beyond city limits. Our hearts jumped as my dad made hard stops and honked and yelled at erratic drivers. Eventually we'd pass under a large green sign that read: BUEN VIAJE, BIENVENIDOS A MÉXICO.

———————

After days of stuffing our mouths with fresh tortillas and rolling around in the grass, our faces warmed by the sun, we'd carefully pack our bags, making our belongings as neat and as small as possible. If we were bringing anything back with us, be it tortillas or frozen tamales, we were to say that they were gifts for a family member on the other side. We wanted our baggage to look like that of a short trip, and we had excuses and explanations for anything we carried with us. We needed the border patrol to think that we were going to Arizona for only a couple of days to visit family, buy some groceries, and come right back. We dressed impeccably so that the officers would think that we were well-off and therefore be less inclined to question if we should be one of the hundreds of immigrants coming back to the United States after the holidays.

During the car ride back to Nogales, my dad prepared us. "Recuerden," he said, "if the officers ask you where you live, never *ever* tell them that you live and go to school in the United States." By the time we reached the long line of cars waiting their turn at the crossing, my brother and I would have a script ready for anyone who asked.

"What school do you go to?" El Colegio Kino near my grandmother's house.

"Who is your teacher?" La maestra Flores.

"Where do you live?" On la Calzada Avenue with our parents and grandparents.

"Do you live in the U.S.?" No, we're visiting family and shopping!

Fer and I would sit in the back of the car nervously, hoping that the officer would believe my parents when they told him that we were only crossing the border temporarily. We knew that underneath my dad's black T-shirt, he'd be drenched in sweat, anxious and terrified of getting caught or turned away. Sometimes the officer would look at Fer and me in the back of the car, making sure that we were the same kids as the ones on the U.S. passports my parents had handed over.

After a few minutes that felt like hours, the officer would give us the pass and say, "Have a good trip." Once we were rolling away, my mother would look over at my dad, eyebrows knit, and place her hand on his leg. She knew how stressed he got every time we crossed paths with La Migra. Collectively we'd all take deep breaths. The air always felt lighter once we had crossed.

———————

When I finally joined my family in Mexico the summer after my freshman year, the emotional release of seeing them after months apart was short-lived. What I hadn't known was how turbulent the situation between my mom and dad had become. I had always been aware of the ways in which they clashed but had chosen to downplay their conflicts and ignore the details of their fights. I never asked if things got physical because one doesn't ask what one already knows. We shared a history of it—of turmoil, of verbal abuse, of having to one-up one another, always being on the defensive. It didn't take long before I fell back into an inescapable pit of fury and chaos. All the yelling had a psychological effect, and the cycle began with my dad, who had a perpetual need to be right. We were bludgeoned with arguments filled with twisted logic backed up by my dad's side of the family, who supported the way that he acted and the way he was finally putting my mom in her place. They seemed to *like* the way he treated her. I watched as they tried to corner Mom, and then my brother and me by default, into submission.

When Mom tried to leave my dad, she told me she was worried he would try to take Fernando away, knowing I couldn't be used as a pawn in the way he could use my brother, who was still only eight years old.

Throughout it all, Fernando tried to intercede, his small voice piping up. "*Please stop, please.*"

Whenever we were in Mexico together, we'd take the two-hour drive between Caborca and Puerto Peñasco, my mom's childhood home. When my dad was out from under the influence of his parents and siblings, he calmed down and the tension between my parents subsided. Because of this predictable pattern, I knew that Puerto Peñasco would be where I would tell Mom about my plan for the future, one largely based on the fleeting promise a teacher had made.

"Mama, me quiero regresar. I want to go back to the United States," I said. "Mama, there is a teacher, Mrs. Hernandez, who said that I could stay with her if I needed to. I can finish high school in America."

I was worried about getting good grades in Mexico. "I got

straight As, Mom. I'm the best student in my entire class," I continued.

My mom grabbed my thighs tightly, pinching them when she did. "Tienes que regresar. You *have* to go back," she replied. "I didn't have you in the United States for you to not take advantage of it."

After all the years I'd spent living and being schooled in the United States, my mother couldn't envision me living my life in Mexico, going to school in Mexico, enrolling in a state college there. I couldn't, either.

"No te preocupes, Elizabeth, tú te vas a ir," she reassured me. "Don't worry, Elizabeth, you will go back."

Dad also knew that it would be better if I stayed in the United States. After all, he was the one who relocated us there when nothing else had gone according to plan. It was for our education, for our future, and for the chance at greater opportunities. Still, he hesitated, letting his anger and mental strain influence him. For weeks that summer he insisted that I couldn't go back, often making excuses that went against everything he had worked for, everything he taught me. "La niña se va a quedar aquí," he said. "Our little girl will stay here."

I fought back, yelling at my dad and then at my mom, blaming them both. "Can't you understand that I have no future here? I can't read books in Spanish or write essays in Spanish. I'll never get ahead here."

Dad fumed at my lack of restraint, often spitting as he spoke. "School will be fine here; you'll get the hang of it." I wanted him to soften, to understand reason and return to being the dad I had grown up with, the dad who told me that I could do anything. Instead, he projected his insecurities about his own marriage on me, I knew that even then. He worried that he'd lose me the way that he was losing my mom.

When the fighting became endless and when my dad continued threatening not to let me go back to the United States, I stopped eating. It was surprisingly easy for me to skip meals and stay in bed. My stomach grew tight, knotting into itself. Eventually I convinced myself to push longer, wondering how long I could go without consuming something. Doing this gave me something to focus on, something to distract me from the uncertainty of the situation, of my family. It gave me a sense of control.

Days turned into weeks and my mom became increasingly worried, bringing me food to my bed after I refused to get up. Slowly, I let the pain from my hunger mix with the pain from my sadness and anxiety.

"Por favor, Elizabeth, please eat," she begged. I looked into her eyes, tired and swollen. She'd been crying. I rarely saw her cry, but every once in a while she'd disappear, and I knew she was crying. I knew because I disappeared to cry, too. It was during those moments, when I saw the sadness in her eyes, that I wanted to give in and end my hunger strike. I wanted to savor the sweetness of the Popsicle she offered; I wanted to embrace my mother, my father, my little brother. I wanted to let them know that I'd stay with them and that we could try, once again, to be a family together.

Certainly it would be hard to let your fifteen-year-old go into a foreign country by herself to live with strangers. I recognized that it would be even harder for my parents because they could never come and see me. If anything bad happened over there, if there was ever an accident, I'd be alone. I knew that I'd be leaving my brother within the wreckage of what was left of our parents' marriage. Even though my dad had spent much of his life fixing everything broken, his relationship with my mom was not a totaled car in a subastas that he could repair. He couldn't fix the way machismo punished, destroyed, and caused toxicity to erupt in our family. I knew that my brother might be collateral damage.

While I wanted to go back to school in America with every fiber of my being, I still loved my dad with all my heart. At night, I tossed and turned. My dreams were filled with violence and terror. In the middle of the night, I'd wake up and find myself— head pounding from hunger and dehydration—with tears running down my face onto a damp pillow. Quietly, I'd turn to my brother, who slept next to me.

"It will all be okay," I'd whisper to him, long after he'd already gone to sleep.

———

At some point in the middle of that summer, I got lice. Nasty little shits that crawled up my head and made my already unstable mood worse. That, combined with the side effects of starvation, resulted in irritability and anger. I dumped it all on my mom as she brushed my hair, parting it little by little to look for lice. I worried that I'd never be able to pursue the life that I dreamed of having, worried that I'd never get to go to college, worried that they'd have to shave all my hair off.

While Mom plucked and poured vinegar onto my burning head, I had time to think about every stupid decision that my parents had made up until then. I began to scream at my mother, excoriating her for not doing enough to save our family, for triggering my dad when she could hold back instead. She listened intently, quietly continuing the tedious work of delousing my thick hair. When my dad came in to check on us, I lashed out at him for his insufferable personality. I hated that he always needed to be right, so I fought to prove him wrong. I hated that they'd come back to Mexico. I was angry that they hadn't done more to stay in the United States, even if it was illegal. I despised the bugs living on my head and the anxiety living in it. I hated that I had worked so hard to be who I was in school in America and he wasn't letting me go back. Every argument gave me the chance to vanquish him and to embolden and empower myself. My brother and cousins kept their distance. The whole house seemed to quake as I began to embody the volatility I'd inherited, turning into an image of what I grew up seeing.

Later that day, Mom tried to coax me, yet again, with food. Once again, I snapped at her. She turned to face my father, who stood at the door, his hands in fists and his lips pursed.

Scowling at him, she said, "You're killing her. You are going to kill her." She stalked out of the room and Dad remained silent, staring at the ground. I hadn't eaten properly in weeks or done much to get out of bed except to treat the damn lice. I was slowly wilting into the mattress, becoming smaller and smaller. After several minutes of silence, he looked up at me, his tense jaw loosening as if he'd broken free from some sort of spell, the shame washing over his face.

"Perdón, mija, you'll go back. We'll drive you back to the United States. I promise," he said. "Todo va a estar bien. It will all be okay."

13

THE GATE

The night before I went back to Arizona, my mind stopped racing. My biggest fear had been having to stay in Mexico, and now that my return was guaranteed, I could relax. At dinner, I slowly spooned food into my mouth, the texture of it still making me slightly sick after not eating well for so long. Once I was done, I hugged my little brother good night and went to bed. I slept like I hadn't in a long time—worried still, but ultimately at peace. The next morning I tried not to acknowledge the fact that I was leaving my family. I took my time with my breakfast, serving myself freshly cut mangoes and papaya, indulgently letting the liquid from the ripe fruit dribble down my face.

"I'll get the napkins," my dad said. His tone was one of great urgency, as if making himself useful would momentarily block out the thought that I was leaving to live under a stranger's roof. "She's a teacher," I'd pleaded. "She's nice and I'll be safe."

"I hope you're right," he'd reply. "No quiero que te pasa nada."

When I finally got up from the kitchen table, I headed to the shower, where my mind raced with different possibilities of how everything would unfold. I felt a tickle in my stomach, but I couldn't figure out if it was excitement or fear. When I got out, I dressed and packed quickly—easy to do because there wasn't much to grab. Most of my belongings at that point were locked in storage rooms that we'd never go back to.

As I walked outside to put my backpack in the car, I was jolted back to reality. My suitcase was the only one in the trunk. My brother and parents had no need to pack bags for themselves. Quickly, I closed the trunk and took my brother's hand, trying to overlook the fact that I'd be alone soon.

"Vamos al Oxxo?" I asked and smiled, nudging him to the corner store across the street. Fernando grinned, forgetting about how big his new adult teeth looked, oversize in his small face. Across the street in the convenience store, I picked out some of my favorites—spicy chips, tamarind candy, and grapefruit soda. I kept looking over, watching Fer eye various things before he grabbed several snacks. His taste was different from mine. He wanted everything sweet: chocolate-filled Pingüinos, sweet breads, milk chocolate. He lugged them all over for the cashier to ring up. The last time we were in Mexico together, he could barely see over the counter; now he towered above it. The thought of him growing up without me made me uneasy. Would he look different every time I visited?

The woman at the register smiled at him and asked, "How are you, Fernando?" I hated that she knew his name and not mine. I wondered how many trips my brother had already made to the Oxxo. Maybe once a day, to pick up the newspaper for my grandfather. Maybe twice a day if he felt like dropping in for a cold soda or a snack. It hadn't taken that long for him to become a regular. When we left the store, I watched out for cars as we crossed the street, warning my little brother to be careful. Instead, he sprinted across, his cargo shorts hiding his rapidly growing legs. He had already spent six months in Mexico without me. He knew the streets of Mexico better than I ever would.

Every time we took long trips, my dad inspected the car and my mom made sure we had sneakers on. "You never know when you'll need to run from a car. The roads are dangerous here," she'd say. That day, under the watchful eyes of my two paternal grandparents, my abuela Delia and abuelo Marcelino, who'd come to say goodbye, my dad checked the car's engine and tires, but Mom didn't remind us about the sneakers.

Instead, she waited in the passenger seat, staring blankly ahead, leaving the door open to let the breeze in. Her eyes, usually bright and animated, were dim. While she knew that she'd lose me soon, she was also preoccupied with the thought of spending three hours with my dad in a closed car. She worried that something would trigger his rage, so her mind raced, trying to come up with escape plans for whatever scenario might come up. It was all she could do to protect us. I watched what had become of my parents, what was becoming of my family, and felt guilty that Fer was witnessing what was once stable dissolve under the extreme duress of my parents' inevitable separation. *He's only eight years old,* I kept thinking to myself.

Next to the car, my grandfather remained quiet, and my grandmother had tears in her eyes. Although they'd always criticized their son, they sided with him during his fits of rage and again after my mom said she didn't want anything to do with my dad or with his family. My grandmother's tears felt forced and performative. Why cry now after inflicting so much pain? Still, I wished that things had been different. I wished that my dad could exhibit the same patience in relation to us as he did in trying to please his own parents. Deep down, I knew that my parents weren't bad people. They were flawed and hurting, and they were human. Humans who needed space to heal. I told myself I needed space, too, and that finally I would have it. I made peace with what it would cost. I had no other choice.

When my dad looked up from the car, he smiled at me, his eyes warm. "Lista?" he said. "Say goodbye to your grandparents, it's time." My grandmother cried and hugged me tight. My grandfather held my hand firmly, looked me in the eyes, and instructed, "Pórtate bien, mija, be good."

"Yo siempre me porto bien, Abuelo. I always behave myself, Grandpa."

———————

I knew that *this* drive up north to Nogales would be unlike any earlier trip. This time, my parents didn't have visas. They wouldn't have to answer to border patrol officers or worry about what we could and couldn't say. That was a relief. But this time, I was the only one going through to the other side—without my parents, without my brother. The reality of not knowing when I'd see them again was unbearable, so I looked out the window, distracting myself with what I did know. I marveled at the winding roads we took up to the United States as I always had. I found comfort in the burn of the hot sun on my face and in the blur of the passing landscape. I watched as we passed through various small towns in northern Mexico—places like Pitiquito, Magdalena, and Santa Ana. Little towns with ancient white churches with symmetrical arches and wooden doors.

Most travelers going north are unaware of the history of these towns. Instead, in a hurry to get to their destination, they skip over them on express highways or pass through without ever stopping to think about the generations of people that built them, that live in them. But my dad, on this trip, chose the slow route, taking his time as we drove through each town, letting us roll our windows down and enjoy the sights of old Mexico to the soundtrack of the subtle thumping of our tires on old cobblestone roads.

My parents taught me about these towns, filling my imagination with pictures of the past. I learned that in the centuries before the churches were built, these small cities and the surrounding areas belonged to the Desert People, the Tohono O'odham, and the River People, the Akimel O'odham. They raised crops, took care of their families, and cultivated their communities along rivers that had long since dried up. Rivers that had once connected to the one I'd grown up near.

The history of the native people was beyond rich. Years after the Spanish came, they maintained their roots and customs, rejecting colonialism and assimilation for as long as they could, resenting the threat that these posed. But in the same way that the dry wind carves out pieces of old houses, customs changed with the arrival of the new people, overriding these ancient cultures.

Over the years, a missionary known as Father Kino established the white churches I'd grown up seeing. They dotted the

Sonoran Desert, creating a route followed by believers and historians like a pilgrimage. For many, these churches were seen as prime examples of European architecture. The willful ignorance of the impact that the O'odham had had on these houses of worship was systemic. Many chose to forget the violence inflicted on the O'odham and the battles that had been fought between the Indigenous communities and the Spanish colonizers. Still, the unmistakable touch of the O'odham was visible between the lines in the careful, traditional ways the clays were mixed to create the church walls.

By the early nineteenth century, the O'odham faced a cruel new reality when the border between the United States and Mexico cut through the land that they had always known as home and started to separate families and communities, further erasing their freedom of movement. On our long car ride, I found myself thinking about how the O'odham community was stripped of choice, of family, and of unity. I thought about how they must have had to go back and forth to see the people that they loved, skirting the law to do what they had once done freely. I thought about the injustice of it all and how, decades later, the same forces that kept trying to break the O'odham seemed to be trying to do that to me.

———————

When we finally arrived at Nogales, my dad navigated his way, as he had always done, through the chaotic city streets. His eyes were tired and somber, his crow's-feet visible more than normal as he squinted into the sun. He parked the car near the border wall, close enough for me to get to the gate and walk across. I sat for a moment before taking my seat belt off, watching him lock the steering wheel in the same way he had when we went to South Tucson. I felt the heaviness of my backpack as I rolled it onto my shoulders, and I let my dad help me with my suitcase for as long as he could.

My mom, my brother, my dad, and I all walked together, raising dust into the air with every step as we got closer to the border entrance, where they'd turn around. During the drive up, Fer had been laughing over nothing, then sleeping, his head bobbing up and down until it rested on my shoulder. But when I looked over at him for the last time, his face crumpled with big, heavy tears. I knelt down and pulled his small body close to mine, hugging him tightly, my sleeve becoming damp with his snot and tears. I remember how cheated I felt not to have had the chance to say goodbye to him when he left the United States in the spring. But I wasn't sure which was worse: not being given an opportunity to say goodbye or being given the chance and still choosing to leave.

Before letting him go I said, "Fernando, te prometo que voy a regresar. Chiquito, I promise that I'll be back." As I hugged my dad, I felt him heaving.

"Por favor, mija, cuídate mucho, please take care of yourself. I love you so much," he repeated.

My mom kept herself together, holding me tight right before I walked across. "Elizabeth, remember that you are strong," she said. I nodded as she pulled my brother up from the ground where he had been sitting on his knees, his face blotchy and red. I admired my mother's ability to stay strong. She was gentle with Fer, wrapping him into her arms tightly.

I walked away from my family mechanically, making it to the

front of the line faster than I would have liked. The border entrance for pedestrians was housed in a large building attached to the long structure made for those crossing by car. It was set up like the security gates in an airport, with machines that scanned luggage. As I got closer to the officer at the front of the line, I blinked away the tears that I'd been holding back and took deep breaths to calm myself down. I didn't want the officer to see the pain inflicted by the institution he worked for.

As my turn came, I resolved not to let my fear of the officers or of ICE take control of me. I was a citizen, and that was something indisputable, something they couldn't take away. When I handed the agent my identification, he glanced down at me, comparing my face with the photo to make sure that I was the same girl. He closed the booklet and asked me where I was going. It was standard procedure, but for some reason, his question was triggering. Why should he care or be entitled to know where I was going within the United States?

I took a deep breath and looked directly into his eyes.

"I'm going home."

PART TWO

14

UNWELCOME CREATURES

The first time that my parents ever saw Merva and Mrs. Hernandez face-to-face was through the border gates, where they waited for me to cross over. Before then, they'd had only a couple of phone calls where they discussed the logistics of my move. On those calls, my dad didn't talk or ask much; he simply nodded and repeated, "Okay, okay." For the most part, I handled the little details, serving as an intermediary between my parents and the adults who would be replacing them as my caregivers.

"Are you sure you trust these people?" my mom asked.

"Yes, Mom, Mrs. Hernandez is a teacher at Richardson," I said. "She's safe—plus Merva even helped us get a lawyer," I continued. "She did that all for free and said she'd be there for me if I ever needed anything." From the look in Mom's eyes, I could tell that she was worried.

"Never give anyone your full trust," she instructed. "Te tienes que cuidar, you have to take care of yourself."

The reality was that I didn't know why my parents were comfortable with me going off with people who were essentially strangers, and that fact didn't truly hit me until I walked away from my family and toward Merva and Mrs. Hernandez, who waved while Merva looked off toward my parents. I watched my dad from a distance, arms crossed, staring down the situation, his gaze fixed on Merva and Mrs. Hernandez like a warning.

I watched Merva smile meekly and wave him off before turning to me, well aware of the heaviness of the situation. Mrs. Hernandez, on the other hand? She was unfazed—unaware of the weight she'd agreed to carry. Her lack of concern should have made me wary, but in that moment I shrugged it off, hoping that it was simply a sign of confidence in the arrangement. All I wanted was to go to school while adding as little as possible to the Hernandez family's plate. Plus, I was accustomed to—and even good at—carrying the weight myself.

———

There was nothing special about the Hernandezes' home. They had a typical driveway surrounded by drought-resistant gravel for landscaping. The inside was also plain, the beige walls and veneer shelves decorated with family pictures of Mrs. Hernandez, her husband Eddie, and their two daughters: Stacy and Melissa. Both girls looked like Mrs. Hernandez—they had her smile and straight hair—but their styles were different. Stacy wore skinny jeans and a beanie; Melissa wore a floral dress and a headband. Eddie loomed over all of them, much taller and quite bald. *They look happy,* I thought to myself the first time I examined them. *Just an ordinary family.* I wasn't surprised by the sameness—this neighborhood was familiar to me. Richardson was within walking distance, and I could point to former classmates' houses where I had gone to sleepovers. Everything was nice, middle class—and on the other side of the river. Even in its plainness, it was everything my parents had wanted for our family. In some ways I felt as if I'd finally made it, just not in the way that I'd always hoped for.

I arrived at the Hernandez home with an itch on my head, upending the calm and composed state I had tried so hard to achieve, or at the very least fake, on the drive over. I told myself that my scalp was itching because it was irritated from all the lice treatment it had endured in Mexico. I was petrified at the thought of having to tell them that I might have brought lice with me.

While Mrs. Hernandez gave me a tour of the house, I forced myself to stop scratching.

"The room down the hall is Stacy's, and ours is right across from it if you ever need anything," she said as she guided me down the corridor. "The room closest to ours is Melissa's—she's away for college and doesn't really live here anymore." I felt my heart flutter as I thought to myself, *Will I have my own room? Could that even be possible?*

I don't know if Mrs. Hernandez realized I'd never had a room that was completely mine. Maybe she saw the hope fill my eyes and thought it best to quickly squash it before I could begin imagining how I would decorate it.

"You'll be sleeping here on the couch for now," she instructed. "I want to keep Melissa's room empty for whenever she comes back."

I forced a smile and said, "Thank you," again and again as she explained the house rules:

- No going out after 6 P.M.
- No hanging out at the park.
- No bringing friends over without cleaning the house first.
- The dishes must be soaked; don't let the water run.
- No watching TV before finishing homework.
- No learning how to drive.

I restrained the part of me that wanted to snap back and question everything, the way I always did, including the part of my mind that wondered why Melissa needed her own room when she had her own apartment while attending a college not even twenty minutes away. Instead, I remembered what my parents had always said whenever they had to live through something uncomfortable. "Remember, Elizabeth, en alguien tiene que caber la prudencia, one must always find a way to be prudent." Big words that essentially meant, "Sometimes you gotta suck it up."

So prudently I kept quiet and followed Mrs. Hernandez through the halls, taking note to avoid what was off-limits. I'd lived with people before, but this time was different. For the rest of my time with the Hernandez family, I would have to make myself smaller. I had to make myself as close to invisible as possible so that I would not become a burden in their lives—an extra cost, an extra mouth to feed, an extra teenager to take to school. They had opened their home to me, and in doing so, they kept my future open. My pursuit of education, my dream of going to college, of making a better future for my family—all of this was still a possibility because of them. I couldn't risk messing it up.

Once Mrs. Hernandez was done showing me around, she mentioned that she had to run out. I meekly asked if I could invite my school friend Desere over. I hadn't seen her in months, and I was desperate for a familiar face.

"Sure, she can come over to say hi for a *little* while," she said. "Just make sure to turn off the alarm system *before* you let her in." I nodded as she motioned toward the little keypad next to the front door. She had shown me how to disarm it during the tour, but being hypervigilant, I watched her again as she headed out, first entering the numbers, 4137, followed by the # sign, and then opening the door. I was desperate to commit the sequence to memory, to not mess up. Neither the trailer nor el cuartito had ever had an alarm system; I don't think I had ever even seen one before. Most people I knew had a dog and hoped for the best. In fact, up until then, I thought alarm systems were something only white people had.

I smiled and waved as I watched Mrs. Hernandez head to her car. As soon as she was out of sight, I ran to the bathroom. My head was still itching, and while I knew that it could be from the hot vinegar my aunt had poured on it to get rid of the lice, I knew that it could also be the bugs themselves. Carefully, I parted my hair down the middle, hoping to find a patch of tender red skin. Instead, I found a fat little vermin, crawling through my hair happily after hitching a free ride to the U.S. of A. I felt myself turn hot as humiliation ran through my body.

As I picked at my scalp, I wondered what the Hernandez family would think of me. They'd be disgusted, I was sure. They'd question why they'd brought me here in the first place. They'd see me as a dirty immigrant girl. It didn't matter how hard my family tried to stay kempt and put together. It didn't matter how much time we'd spent hoping to project a positive impression to others in a foreign country. A good kid doesn't get lice. A good immigrant doesn't get lice. But there I was, with a head full of it.

As I scratched my head, I thought about the times when my mom did my hair before I went to school, pulling hard and gelling it down into clean ponytails. "No quiero que parezcas una pordiosera," she'd say. "We don't want you to look like you're homeless." Back then, I'd growl and complain about the pain—not caring about what people might think when they saw me.

I guess I am homeless, I thought to myself as I stared at my disheveled hair and wrinkled clothes in the mirror. Quietly, I grabbed my brush and put my hair up into a tight bun, wondering if I'd disappointed my mother by falling into the stereotype she'd worked so hard for me to avoid.

In the months and even years that followed, I knew that I would be seen in one of two ways. On one end of the spectrum, there was the narrative of the super-immigrant—the newly arrived person who strives to be the best, who assimilates and somehow overcomes everything that comes between them and success. Society loves these immigrants, praising them and benefiting from their contributions. These are the immigrants that we idolize as the ideal symbols of American success, as achievers of the elusive American dream.

On the other end of the spectrum are the immigrants people use as scapegoats. They're laborers and dishwashers. They're the janitors in my high school, my uncle and aunt, my mom and dad.

They're people who come across good opportunities. They're the immigrants people hate and talk shit about straight to my face. They're the immigrants that white people love to tell me that I am not like. "Oh, but not you," they say. "You're such a smart girl."

I'd learned to smile a lot through gritted teeth, keenly aware of the ways in which I was perceived. It's not hard to tell which version of the immigrant I strived to be. *Elizabeth, tú tienes que ser el mejor, you have to be the best.* But here I was, mere months after getting my transcript with that glorious number one ranking in the bottom corner, in a home that was not my own, with a family that was not my own, looking in the mirror at a face I did not recognize, and holding a fucking dead bug in my hand that twenty seconds ago was living off my head. I was not Mexico's best.

Desere knocked on the front door, interrupting my self-sabotaging train of thought. I hurried to the door, stopping to enter 4137# on the keypad. Opening the door, I was struck by how grateful I felt to see a face I knew, the face of a person I felt like I had known in another life—a life that was somehow only three months ago.

Desere plopped down on the couch that doubled as my bed, and I slowly and carefully sat down, strategically keeping my gross head as far away from the back of the couch as possible. She hadn't been there long when there was another knock on the door. I remember briefly hesitating to answer it because it wasn't my house, but then again, I was living here. We decided it was probably okay to answer it, but I couldn't have anticipated opening the door to two white police officers.

I stood there, my face flushed as adrenaline ran through my body. I waited for the cops to say something while a million thoughts crossed my mind. My immediate reaction was fear of the authorities, of what they could do to my family—deportation, incarceration, or worse. The fear was followed by relief as I remembered that my parents weren't there. There was no need to cover up, protect, or defend the status of my family. Finally I remembered what my dad always used to tell me: "Tú eres ciudadana. You have rights, and you can use them." Mentally I reassured myself that the cops couldn't do anything to me. I didn't have anything else that they could take away.

The police officers took a second to assess me and Desere, who peeked her head from the couch.

"We got a notice from your security system. Is everything okay?" one of them asked. I could see the alarm keypad from the corner of my eye. Apparently, I hadn't disarmed the alarm system as well as I thought. Calmly, I explained to the officers that I must've not turned it off properly, letting them know that I lived there and hoping that they would believe me. The two seemed satisfied with my response and turned around. Once they were gone, I worried about how Mr. and Mrs. Hernandez were going to respond, since the alarm company had called them as well.

Within hours, I had already fucked up. Having lice and inadvertently calling the cops were not ways to be small.

After Mrs. Hernandez got home, there was a brief lukewarm lecture on the alarm system followed by my lice confession. For a moment I felt like I was back at church—sermons and confessionals, complete with crucifixes on the wall. Thankfully my anxiousness subsided when Mrs. Hernandez, who was now insisting I call her Diane, assured me that it was no big deal, and that Eddie, whom I wanted to still call Mr. Hernandez, would pick up lice shampoo for me on his way home from work. I hated being a charity case, but I hated having lice more.

That night, the Hernandez family ate dinner somewhat in shifts, heating up microwavable food at different times. I ate a bowl of cereal with Eddie, I don't know when Diane ate, and Stacy came home later, well after 6 P.M., and briefly greeted me while grabbing a Hot Pocket. The contrast was stark to how my family, my culture, would have welcomed a guest into our home. But everything about that first day felt strange.

Before settling in that night, I had to deal with what had settled on my head. In Mexico my mom and aunt had helped me comb every strand of my thick black hair, but in the Hernandez house, I had to do it all by myself. The shampoo tingled and stung as it penetrated my scalp, and I tried as best I could to comb all the hairs on the back of my head. It took me forever, but I managed to get all the lice out. Once I was done, I walked down the hallway and flopped down on the couch where I would sleep. I was out as soon as my head hit the pillow.

I woke up abruptly the next morning as if I'd experienced a nightmare. For the first few seconds, I panicked and forgot where I was as my eyes adjusted to the unfamiliar things around me. The beige living room, the pictures of a family that wasn't mine. I shuddered at the sight of my own shadow, letting what felt like an electric current run down my spine. I wondered if the nightmare that I'd had was worse than the one I'd woken up to. Everything felt foreign. *I* felt foreign, like an impostor of a citizen.

I wasn't home, but then again, I wondered what *home* even meant for me anymore.

15

HUNGER

Despite a rocky start, my first few weeks at the Hernandez home were filled with a state of cautious excitement. Initially I didn't mind the lack of freedom I felt under their unfamiliar and irrational house rules. I had already lost the freedom to be with my family, so not going out after 6 P.M., not learning to drive, and avoiding the park didn't feel like a big deal in comparison. The Hernandez family also didn't give me any money, and I didn't blame them. It's not like it mattered; I'd never been materialistic—it was hard to be when I didn't have anything to begin with. Plus, Diane and Eddie had both welcomed me with open arms, gave me a couch to sleep on, asked me to join them for fast-food trips, and took me with them to Walmart. They liked to sit with me in the living room, sometimes telling me stories about God. The Hernandezes rarely ate meals together, which confused me because my mom had always told me that only gringos didn't eat together. I had never known a Mexican

family not to share meals. They didn't speak Spanish to one another, either. But then again, they had been Americans for more
generations than I had. It made me wonder if they knew Spanish
and chose not to speak, or if they'd lost the language altogether.

Sometimes Eddie and I would eat bowls of whatever was left
over at the table together. He often made a ground beef and
canned vegetable concoction that we covered in ketchup and
ate by the spoonful. (Maybe they *were* gringos after all . . .) While
the ground beef mush was heavy on my stomach and not the
worst thing I'd ever eaten, hanging with Eddie was always fun.
He was less serious than Diane, and time spent with him could
be enjoyable even if I had to put up with a little God talk some
of the time.

At school, Stacy would go out during lunch in her car with
friends. She was popular, and I loved getting a treat from her
whenever she came back. Sometimes it was a bag of Chicken
McNuggets from McDonald's; other times, it was a meal from ee-
gee's, a local Tucson chain known for its frozen ice. Whenever she
brought me back something to eat, I felt *cool*. I felt *American*. I felt
like I belonged.

I don't know when the honeymoon phase of living with their
family began to wear off. Maybe it was when I'd come home sore
from soccer or tennis practice and so tired from school that I'd
sit on the floor of the kitchen and open the fridge to find nothing. Maybe it was when Diane made it clear that she wished I
wouldn't participate in so many extracurricular activities, because she couldn't shuttle me to and from them, even when I
always figured out my own rides. Maybe it was when they stopped
taking me on their fast-food trips, coming back with only food

for themselves. Maybe it was when Stacy adopted a kitten, shifting everyone's attention from the teenager on the couch to the small furry creature's blue eyes. Maybe it was when the novelty of Diane telling her religious friends that she "took in a girl so she could finish high school because her parents can't come back to the United States" wore off. Maybe it was when I realized they offered to take me in but not necessarily to take care of me.

At the end of most days, I was hungry. The pit in my stomach reminded me of how I felt during Sunday mass—which would last from eleven in the morning well into lunchtime—back when my mom used to make us all go. Depending on the priest's sermon, the clock kept ticking further and further past lunch, making it increasingly difficult to follow what already felt dry and tedious. My hunger would grow along with my annoyance at the priest's broken, non-native-speaking Spanish. I could feel every part of my body twitch as I desperately tried to sit still. My mom would shoot me looks when she could hear my stomach tighten and groan. If I was really hungry, I even craved going up for communion. Despite the fact I doubted the meaning behind it all, the small, round piece of bread was something. But the body of Christ never satisfied my hunger. What it *did* do was signal the end of church.

Afterwards, my parents would throw around lunch options and we'd usually settle on the Panda Express next to the highway. Orange chicken and fried rice were our Sunday staples. My parents always got forks while I got chopsticks, convinced I needed to practice for a life in which I would get to use them more often. I visualized fancy sushi in Japan or maybe a trip to China. We would laugh and pick from one another's food. The hunger I felt in church never lasted because I knew we would eat together soon. And then of course, I had learned to weaponize my body's need for food, wielding the power of my hunger to get my parents to agree to let me come back to the United States after their visas were denied.

Maybe the honeymoon phase at the Hernandezes' wore off when my hunger—which at one point evoked memories of being together with my family—became a harsh reminder of our separateness.

For a while I made do during school lunch by eating what my friends didn't finish from their trays. Angelica and Nancy never pressured me into talking about why I didn't have my own food. Sometimes my friend Alex drove us down the street in her ugly PT Cruiser (aka the PT Loser) to get hot dogs. They never made it awkward or uncomfortable. Instead, they'd split their fries with me or give me some loose change to use at the school's vending machines. I looked forward to the expired honey buns rolling off the rusted metal coil. I savored every bite into the greasy melted bun heated up by the Arizona sun. My friends knew my situation was complicated and that the Hernandez family was complicated. They also knew my hunger was complicated.

My parents tried sending me money whenever they could, but their money felt tainted, like something I shouldn't have the right to use when I was the one who wanted to leave. It didn't help that any money sent was followed by long soliloquies from my dad, usually through Facebook Messenger. "I'm sorry that I can't send more, I'm sorry for all of this," he'd write. For a long time, I stared at the blue messages on the computer screen while a mixture of guilt and anger danced in my stomach. I was angry at my parents for their fighting and childishness. I was angry at the ways they added another fissure in our already cracked family as their marriage disintegrated. I was angry that I couldn't tell them that I was using the money they sent to buy cereal because it was cheap and lasted for a long time, that I would add water and a banana to the cereal and blend it into some sort of disgusting excuse for a smoothie. I was angry that I couldn't tell them I was hungry.

"Be prudent, Elizabeth."

I tried to remember how lucky I was to have been taken in by this family.

I have a roof over my head, I am grateful.

I am on their family healthcare plan for emergencies. If there is an emergency, I will be grateful.

I may be hungry, but I am not starving. I am grateful.

Do. Not. Complain.

Eventually, I avoided answering my parents' phone calls and messages, ignoring them as they piled up in my inbox unread. When I did pick up the phone, my mom would apologize, too.

"I miss you, mi chiquitita," she'd say.

"I miss you, too, Mom, but I gotta finish my schoolwork, okay?" I'd hear my mother pause quietly. I'd listen to her faint breathing over the crackling speaker, remembering the times that I'd press my ear to her belly when she was pregnant with my brother, my face rising and falling with her breath. Eventually, she'd clear her throat.

"Está bien, te cuidas, mi corazón." When she hung up, I'd sit still on the floor, surrounded by unfinished homework, blinking as much as possible to keep the tears inside.

Sometimes Diane would find me there and ask, "Hey, you okay?"

I tried avoiding her gaze. "Yep! Going to go shower!" I'd reply, quickly grabbing some of my schoolwork and putting it away.

"Okay, make sure no one else needs that bathroom first, and can you pick this stuff up so it's not in the way?" she'd ask, stepping over notebooks as she headed into the kitchen.

Maybe the honeymoon phase wore off when I started crying in the shower, letting the hot water burn my skin as I sat in the tub.

Maybe it was when I realized that a person could go hungry in the land of abundance.

Over the next few months, I started to struggle in class. I had pressured my school counselors to put me in advanced courses, begging them to stack my schedule, assuring them I was smart enough and more than capable. The thing with those classes is that they are usually really quiet. It was then when my hunger would speak to me most, forcing me to listen and drawing unwanted attention my way. My hunger was rude, making itself known at the most inopportune moments. Outside of the quiet classroom walls, I could live with hunger and sometimes even forget about it. But when hunger decided to speak and others started to hear it, things got more complicated.

Hunger was the most vocal during math, thriving in Mr. Becker's cool, dimly lit classroom as he projected lesson plans onto the whiteboard. Sometimes Nikolina would look over at me, waving her hand. "Hey, Liz, I have a granola bar if you want it," she'd say.

"Thanks," I'd reply, grateful for her kindness.

After class, Mr. Becker would do the same, offering me a bag of popcorn as I headed out. "You know, popcorn is a great brain food," he'd say, waving me off as hunger and I went on to our next class.

I don't know who told the school counselors about what I had going on, but eventually they found out. I figure Mr. Becker or Mrs. Lopez, our anatomy teacher who was also my friend Desere's mom, told on me. They were the kind of teachers who would worry about the kid in their class who was always hungry or the kid who had to sit up front in the class because her eyesight was terrible and she didn't have the glasses she needed.

When I got a slip one day in class asking me to come into the guidance counselor's office, I figured it was to discuss my schedule. The counselors at my high school knew me well, but they never saw me as a kid with problems. They knew me as the straight-A student who always requested advanced courses, participated in sports, joined and started clubs, and was "so smart" and "mature" for my age. When I got to the main office, I was directed to Mrs. Trejo, who offered me a Snickers bar as I sat down.

Mrs. Trejo was a sweet older lady with a short gray bob. Calm, gentle, and kind, she reminded me of my great-aunts in Mexico. She had a corner office with warm lighting. Her wall, like the rest of the counselors' walls, was full of pictures from students who had graduated, students that had come and gone through her many years of service. What I didn't know was that Mrs. Trejo was a social worker.

"Elizabeth, I've heard that you're living with Stacy Hernandez's parents. Is that true?"

When she asked this, I shrugged. "Yeah. It's all right, though. My parents aren't in the United States right now," I explained. "I don't know if they'll ever be able to come back, but it's no big deal."

Mrs. Trejo was patient, almost too patient. Her slow-paced questions were in contrast to my rapid convoluted answers. "And we have the Hernandezes listed as your guardians. Is that correct?" she wondered.

"Yes, they are, along with Merva Bridges, who is listed in case of emergencies." I kept rambling. "Between Merva and Diane, documents were notarized, and a lawyer was contacted to help with the nitty-gritty." As she jotted things down in the notebook in front of her, I squirmed, trying to stop my leg from shaking.

"Are you on the free lunch plan?" she asked.

"No, I'm not anymore," I said, laughing nervously. I had been on it when I lived with my parents, but because the Hernandez family was middle class, I didn't think I qualified anymore. Their daughter Stacy wasn't on it, so why would I be?

"Okay, well, we're going to get you signed up for that right away," she continued. "You don't have to use it if you don't want to, but you're eligible."

I nodded in silence. "Is it only for lunch or do I get breakfast, too?" I asked, still guarded.

"You can get breakfast, too. We can set you up to ride one of the early buses to get you here before class and you'll be all set." I felt simultaneously relieved and embarrassed. I would have something to eat. And I was a charity case . . . again.

"You're also eligible for a program that might be helpful for you," she said. "It's called Youth On Their Own—YOTO, for short—and it's an organization that helps students in situations like yours."

It was then when I learned that I was considered a homeless, at-risk student. Mrs. Trejo explained that it didn't matter that the Hernandez family had guardianship over me. I still qualified for the program.

"It might not happen, but you should be aware that arrangements like yours aren't always permanent," she cautioned. "Especially when you're sleeping on the couch." Mrs. Trejo told me that through YOTO, I'd get a monthly stipend of $140. Money my parents couldn't afford to send me. Money I could use for food and clothes. I would have access to a pantry that YOTO had across the street from the school. It had food like cereal and canned soup, and it had products like deodorant and tampons. Outwardly hesitant but inwardly excited, I gave her the okay to sign me up for it.

"Elizabeth, I want you to know that you can always come to me or anyone else in this office for help," she said, guiding me toward the door. I nodded back at her as I left, embarrassed and grateful. Mrs. Trejo never told the Hernandez family about our interaction or about the fact that she'd signed me up for YOTO. For the first time since coming back to the States without my family, I felt like I had people watching out for me, paying attention, noticing what I had forgotten: that despite convincing myself that I was a young adult, I was still a child who needed sustenance; a child who, like all humans, deserved to have her hunger satiated.

16

EARTH CAMP

Getting assistance from Youth On Their Own allowed me to get back on track, to once again hunger for academic achievement and college instead of food. I was even able to get glasses through YOTO and no longer needed to sit at the front of the class to see the board. I could see my future again.

Throughout the rest of my sophomore year, school became more of a home than I ever had with the Hernandez family. And I wondered, if things stayed the same, if it would become more of a home than I ever had—or would ever have again—with my parents.

On one hand, when I was in school, I felt supported. I had adults checking in on me, seeming to care about me above and beyond what my grades were—something I hadn't even learned to do for myself. I knew my parents loved me beyond what was on my report card, but I also knew that they had sacrificed a lot for me to have my citizenship and my education. So while school was predictable and calm in some ways, it was full of pressure and intense in others. But that's what home always was for me, too: predictable, yet full of pressure. I was used to holding multiple truths and multiple worlds at the same time.

Everything I did at school, from studying to soccer to taking AP classes, had an undertone of "this will look good on a college application." But even with that pressure, I still found ways to be creative and have fun; I still found ways to be a kid. In the summer after my sophomore year, I was selected to attend Earth Camp through the Arizona-Sonora Desert Museum. I had always had a love for nature and sustainability, even before I knew what the word *sustainability* meant. When I was little, I'd hear my parents crumpling plastic bags and would come running in from the other room to talk to them about how we *have* to switch to reusable bags to protect the earth. If they pulled out Styrofoam cups, they'd glance at each other knowingly, waiting for "Little Miss Greenpeace," as they liked to call me, to show up and talk about how Styrofoam shrinks in the ocean but never fully disappears and how humans suck for treating the earth so poorly. I don't even remember where my love of nature and taking care of the earth came from. It was almost an innate part of my identity.

During Earth Camp, high schoolers spent twelve days hiking and camping throughout Arizona and Utah, learning about life in the Sonoran Desert, ecology, the value of National Forests, and ways to be good stewards of nature. The first day started off like the typical first day of any overnight camp: your parents drop you off and you say goodbye to them. In other words, it started with me once more being the odd one out. The girl who had to catch a ride with someone else's family, the girl who had already said goodbye to her parents on the other side of the border.

I quickly swallowed the familiar feelings of otherness, focusing instead on my excitement and anticipation. We spent our first day and night in the Desert Museum, getting to know the live animals in the museum, studying native wildflowers, and preparing our packs for the trek ahead. I frantically took notes about everything we were learning. There wasn't going to be a test at the end, but taking notes grounded me. Writing and learning were part of who I was even when school rankings were stripped away. As my parents always said, an education is something that nobody can take away.

We woke up early the next morning and drove over six hours from Tucson to Chinle, into the heart of the Navajo Nation, the ancestral lands of the Diné. Here we would head to the Canyon de Chelly—about two hundred miles east of the Grand Canyon—for our first hike and camp-out. While millions and millions of people visit the Grand Canyon each year, Canyon de Chelly is visited by only a couple hundred thousand. In a society that quantifies worth by the numbers of followers and likes, the relatively unknown nature of the canyon only amplified its sacredness.

Before we could descend into the canyon, we met Wapi, a Navajo man who would guide us on the hike. Wapi still lived along the canyon, raising livestock and harvesting crops just as his ancestors had for thousands of years. Anyone who wanted to hike deep into the canyon needed a Navajo guide because the canyon was on Indigenous land belonging to the Navajo. I was struck by Wapi's calm and his reverent energy, but also by his mere presence standing in front of me. Long before Arizona passed laws erasing my culture from the curriculum, they had wiped out the knowledge of Indigenous cultures, speaking of them only in the past tense, as if they no longer existed—whitewashed in history class and entirely ignored in current events.

Wapi shared with us the history and present-day life of the canyon, stories from the Puebloans, who first discovered that the area was nourished by extensive water sources that created rich soil for crops, to the Hopi, who would later inhabit the land to plant corn and fruit, to his own people, the Diné, who still live there today. He talked somberly about the Long Walk, the attempted ethnic cleansing of his people by the U.S. government. He spoke of peaches, weaving, and peace treaties. He shared with us the history of the land. The rushing streams that shaped the uplifting land, which together created the colorful walls of the canyon. The droughts, the flash floods, the rock art, the homes carved into and out of the very land we walked on. The homes that remind us that the history of the land and the history of the people can never be torn apart; they are one and the same.

The ancient ruins of homes carved into the deep red walls of the canyon were disorienting in their beauty and in their window to the past. It was difficult to imagine the life that was here before, the laughter that once filled the homes. Some of the ruins are known as the White House Ruins, named after the white plaster that was used to build the upper dwelling. They were built thousands and thousands of years before the more recognizable White House that Americans know today.

The canyon became a National Monument under President Herbert Hoover's leadership in 1931, a few decades after the Long Walk. The government wanted to preserve thousands of years of archaeological resources, so now the Navajo worked in partnership with the government, and specifically the National Park Service, to manage the land. It seemed odd to me. Why is it that people who have had their land stolen are forced to befriend the thieves who took it from them? Why is it that people whose families were killed must befriend the murderers in an attempt to continue to live?

Maybe I need to play the game by their rules, I thought, *the same rules that tore my family apart—in an attempt to put us back together. Maybe a hostage must befriend her captor in order to ever taste freedom.*

I wanted to take notes, to keep track of everything I was learning, but the circumstances of the hike—from the distractingly stunning layers of red and orange stone jetting up from the ground below us to the steep terrain and my forty-pound backpack—didn't allow me to. Instead, I soaked up what I could in my mind before the endurance required for the hike forced me to focus on every step, staring down at my thrift-shop hiking boots, watching the kicked-up clouds of red dust settle on my legs until beads of sweat went streaming through the grime—the lines on my Brown skin mirroring the sacred land of the Diné.

On the floor of the canyon, we walked along the muddy stream, learning the chronology of water: the decades when water nourished the harvest into abundance; the periods of drought; the years in which when water was needed, you simply dug your hand into the dirt; the times when flash floods had undoubtedly taken lives. After one woman had drowned in a flash flood, a witness put it this way: "The canyon is thought of as a benevolent entity by those who live there, and people forget it also has a dark and unpredictable side. It can flood so fast you won't even see it coming. Then it's peaceful again . . . Look at it now: blue skies, puffy clouds, horses grazing . . . you'd never know something terrible happened here last night."

We set up camp within the canyon that night, and as I lay in my sleeping bag, I thought of the Rillito River and its unpredictability. I thought of living on my side of the river with my family and finally making it to live on the other side, but without them. I thought of all the times we'd crossed the border into Mexico, ultimately not knowing if we would make it back together to the United States. The number of times we had crossed and were able to cross back made the trip feel routine, normal. But then one day, when I was old enough, I was forced to begin crossing alone. The unpredictability was as much a part of my story as my family, my language and culture, my Brown skin, and my education.

I felt a sense of connection to the Navajo people and to the land that was theirs and yet not entirely theirs. Wapi, his family and his ancestors, the canyon and the earth—they all ebbed and flowed through cycles of drought and floods, good times and bad. They, too, held on to their history and nourished and worried about their future. Would the sacrifices of the generations who came before all be in vain? Would their grandchildren have the right paperwork and know how to participate in the government processes needed to keep their land? Would the powers that be in the government take back the land that they stole in the first place? I knew only too well the fear of paperwork.

I was so exhausted from the hike that my mind couldn't spin for too long before I was fast asleep. I slept better on the floor of the canyon than I ever did on the Hernandezes' couch. The remainder of Earth Camp was spent rafting, camping, hiking in Arches National Park, and touring Glen Canyon Dam. We learned about hydrology, endangered species, fire science, geology, geomorphology, invasive species, and biology. We debated the pros and cons of dams, discussed water-use issues, and had zero-waste challenges.

Were we merely behaving as humans in a capitalist society—finding ways to make a struggle meaningful, to give it some sort of purpose; looking for ways to monetize everything? Or was I simply acting as a slightly obsessive, somewhat neurotic daughter of immigrants who was determined to survive and make a better future for not only my family but for everyone?

Regardless, during Earth Camp I decided that I was going to study political science and environmental science, become a lawyer, and save the planet. No big deal, right? Deep down I felt that if I protected the earth, then I was also protecting people.

People like Wapi and his family, like the other Navajo families that still lived in the canyon. People like my brother, who deserved the level of education and opportunity I was getting, but instead was in Mexico living with the tension and violence of our parents' crumbling marriage. On the drive back to the Arizona-Sonora Desert Museum I wondered why I was the one who got to escape it all while my brother had to stay behind. I wondered about the responsibility I bore to make something *of* myself but never *for* myself. Would my brother ever feel the pressure that I do; would he ever carry the same weight? Does he experience more of the freedom that I crave? The freedom I found in those moments in the depths of the Canyon de Chelly as I stared up at the rock walls and the night sky strewn with stars. The moments of awe, of grueling hard work paying off, of rest and water, of nature and natives, of honoring the past by being present in the now. The moments of freedom that were really nothing more than brief intervals for me.

Ironically, I wanted my brother both to have more freedom than I did and to one day help me carry this weight.

I wondered how Wapi carried it all—how he and his family remained resilient and peaceful, hopeful and optimistic for the future. How he partnered with the system that murdered his people and separated him from his family. I wondered how Wapi survived.

The last day of our trip in the canyon, I learned that Wapi is a Navajo name that means *lucky*. I wondered if Wapi felt lucky.

17

MEXICAN CINDERELLA

Back at the Hernandez house for my junior year, I continued to ride the adrenaline that Earth Camp produced in me. With the help of mentors from the Arizona-Sonora Desert Museum, I immediately started an Earth Club at my school. At first only a couple of kids from chemistry showed up, but eventually we had a full-fledged club of fifteen to organize activities with the museum, go night gazing, and do highway cleanups. Junior year was exciting because I was one step closer to the end goal, one step closer to college. Unlike in past years, it didn't take long to settle into the routine of school and extracurricular activities. By this point, I knew what it took to keep my GPA up, even if it meant I had to shrink myself to fit back onto the couch of a family I couldn't claim. Going back to the Hernandezes' house after school felt like wearing shoes a size too small.

Still, I tried to make myself feel as if I belonged, identifying things I had in common with them. Time and time again,

I found myself drawn to their impressive VHS collection. As a form of escapism from the emptiness I felt without my family, I turned to Disney. Especially after long days at school, I'd pop a classic into the VCR and regress into the beauty and nostalgia of my childhood before the United States.

Although I knew the plots of those movies like the back of my hand, there were still differences between the VHS tapes I had watched when I was a child and the ones I was now borrowing. My childhood versions of the tapes had been entitled *Cenicienta, La Sirenita,* y *La Bella Durmiente.* Now they were *Cinderella, The Little Mermaid,* and *Sleeping Beauty.* The lyrics, the dialogue—everything was flipped and skewed in English. As I watched characters like Timon and Pumbaa get into trouble, I tried to remember if what they said was funnier in Spanish. "They must be," I told myself. "Everything is funnier in Spanish."

One evening after I'd popped in a tape, my mom phoned me. I'd been avoiding calls from both my mom and my dad for weeks, claiming to be too busy. The truth was, I didn't want to hear or get more details about what I already knew. They were officially separating, my parents, and not amicably. Through his tears, my brother had kept me updated on the situation, telling me that he missed me. I always tried to answer his calls.

"Mom moved in with la abuela Chelo," my brother updated me. "Now if I want to see her, she's two hours away."

"It's for the best," I tried to assure him. "When Mom and Dad are together, they fight, and it's never pretty, you know that."

"I know." He sighed. "I just wish you were still here to help me deal with them. I don't know how to make them calm down."

"I'll make it up to you," I teased lightly. "Your ninth birthday is coming up. You're getting old."

As I let the phone ring, I imagined my brother by himself trying to navigate the chaotic feelings of two parents who could no longer make things work. So I answered the phone, hoping to take some of the burden off of his shoulders, hoping that the conversations that I did have with my mom or dad would stay light.

"Cómo estás, mi niña?" my mom whispered, the warmth of her voice coming through over the phone.

"I've been watching movies again," I told her.

"*The Little Mermaid?*" she asked. "That was always your favorite." I could almost feel her there, her eyes crinkling up as she spoke. "We used to get you every mermaid toy possible," she said with a sigh.

I thumped my head back into the couch, remembering the tangled mess of dolls with tails, pretty faces, and hair that changed color underwater. I felt remorse for them, lost somewhere in a dust-covered plastic bag.

"I still like *The Little Mermaid*, but lately I've been more into *Mulan*," I replied.

"Ariel followed her dreams and Mulan saved her family," Mom said on the other line. I wanted to tell her that I watched *Cinderella* more than any of the other films because I was the Mexican Cinderella, living in a home where other people had control over me, where there were different rules for me than for their real children, where I had to clean up after them, where I hadn't felt beautiful since day one (at least Cinderella didn't have lice). Growing up, I watched Disney movies to help me dream, to help me remember the wonder of a different life. Now I watched them to feel less alone, as if my only shot at camaraderie was with a skinny blond-haired girl who used a pumpkin as a getaway car.

"It's getting late. I have to get some homework done before Diane gets mad," I said into the phone.

"Why does she care?" Mom prodded. "You always get everything done." I silently nodded in agreement, thankful that nobody in this house could understand me when I talked shit in Spanish.

"I don't know, Mom," I deflected, not wanting to get into it.

"Okay, baby, te quiero mucho."

"I love you, too."

Speaking to my parents over the phone unsteadied me, but nothing was worse than when my parents passed the phone to Fer. His little voice made my heart shrink like a raisin whenever I heard it.

"Cómo estás, Fernando?" I asked him.

"Bien," he replied with a melancholic sweetness. "I miss my old friends still, but I am making new ones."

"I promise that I'll bring you back," I said. "We won't be apart forever."

"Ya sé, Elizabeth," he replied. "I miss you the most." Though I treasured hearing Fer's voice, my phone conversations with him and with my parents jerked me back to reality. A reality without the time or space for fairy tales.

So I kept my phone calls short and chose to watch movies where girls achieve their dreams with the help of trusty sidekicks who egg them on. I clung to an unverified assumption that getting good grades would somehow lead to my family's salvation. *My* Mexican Cinderella story includes a mother figure who

makes me wash her daughter's dishes, nagging at me to do it a
certain way. She lets her own daughters go out and explore the
world while I stay locked within the four walls of a home I do
not feel welcome in. No one-dimensional princes are on their
way to save me—there's no time for distractions like that. In my
story, I'm doing everything possible to bring my little nine-year-
old sidekick back from Mexico so that we can take on the world
together.

———————

As the movie credits rolled on the TV screen hours later, I
heard Stacy come home briefly to pick up some stuff before heading out again. I watched her drive away with someone
she'd been hanging out with a lot behind Diane's back. I envied
Stacy, who moved through our high school hallways with a careless ease; she was the epitome of effortlessness. A tomboy who
kept her hair short and had her own edgy style, she was popular
and confident.

Stacy and I would occasionally eat Hot Pockets together at
the house, and she'd always say hi to me at school, but for the
most part she did her own thing and I did mine. And our worlds
couldn't have been more different. She got invited to parties,
and I tried to convince kids to come to Earth Club's stargazing night. She smoked socially, and I played tennis awkwardly.
She snuck in make-out sessions, and I snuck spoonfuls of instant
coffee mix to keep me awake to study. She had mastered that
thrown-together-but-still-cool look, and I wondered if people
could smell the chicken grease in my hair from my new job at
KFC, which I'd gotten because it was within walking distance

of the Hernandez house. Stacy always had twenty dollars in her pocket from her mom and dad. She didn't need to work like I did. Instead, she drove her own car around Tucson, blasted music and the air-conditioning carelessly—a practice that made me even angrier after Diane had told me that she didn't want me to learn how to drive. As I sweated my ass off riding a used bike to the public library for weekly college prep meetings, I ran through the productive and totally responsible ways that I would use a car if I had one.

Stacy was also hard to read. I didn't know if she genuinely liked me or if she was nice to me only because I slept on her family's couch, but having her acquaintance and acceptance made me feel cool even if I tried to convince myself that I was too focused on *real* life to concern myself with the social dynamics in high school. Stacy gave me a social currency that I never had time to spend. More than anything, though, her sheer existence pissed me off. Not her personally, but everything her carefree teenage life represented. Every normal teenage thing—every normal *human* thing—she got to experience I had to convince myself was merely an obstacle in the way of my goals. And when I was really bitter, I'd wonder if she even *had* goals, arrogantly assuring myself I was simply too mature to be distracted by the frivolity of normalcy.

We lived different lives and played by different rules. She could stay out late, fail to turn in assignments, pull average grades, and spend money that she hadn't earned. I got in trouble if I wasn't home by sunset (unless I was stargazing with the Earth Club), and I had to do my homework before I could watch TV. Stacy never had to clean as much as I did and wouldn't know the first thing about how to work a washing machine. I was always washing dishes that weren't mine, and I did my own laundry.

One evening Diane was doing Stacy's laundry when suddenly there was a quick shuffling of feet down the hallway. Diane had forgotten to start the dryer, but I didn't care enough to tell her. Within minutes the murmurs in Diane and Eddie's room had become shouts, the tension was rising, and I could sense that the house was about to shake. Had I been with my family, in our own place, this would have been the moment that I slithered into the bedroom to wait out the storm. But when the living room is your bedroom, there's nowhere to escape.

I overheard that Diane had found a love letter in the pocket of Stacy's jeans. I was baffled as to why this caused such urgency in Diane but also intrigued—perhaps the fling Stacy had with Ryan at school was more than a fling. *Come on, Eddie, read it out loud!* I thought to myself as I stared at my homework, pretending to be preoccupied in case they came out of their room.

I could tell Eddie was talking about God, but I couldn't make out what he was saying. He always talked about God, though, so it didn't take long for me to get bored with my eavesdropping and go back to my homework. But then Stacy came home, and the shit hit the fan.

It turned out the love letter was from a *girl* that Stacy had been dating. And turns out super-religious dads aren't down with their children being gay or bisexual or anything but heterosexual.

Over the next several weeks, the tension rose in the house like the pressurized air in the organ pipes at mass, spilling over into the streets at certain times of day.

"This is just a phase!" Eddie yelled as he commanded Stacy to go to church and find God. I thought of catechism and wondered again why religion is such a high-stakes game, one in which the winners get heaven and the losers get . . . well, apparently Eddie wanted Stacy to believe that the losers got love letters from gay kids, as if that's some form of hell.

Diane and Eddie argued as often as Eddie talked about God. Diane seemed torn between her marriage, her religion, and the motherly love she had for her daughter. Stacy mostly cried. I started staying away from the house as much as I could, visiting my uncle on the other side of the river, taking Whiskey for walks, going over to check in with Merva's family, who were much more chill. I even picked up extra shifts at the KFC simply to have an excuse to be out. The later I could be out, the better—it meant only that I needed more instant coffee to stay up and finish my schoolwork.

When I had to be in the house, I crept around like the ill-timed guest that I was, so good at being small and quiet that Eddie was often startled by my presence. "You're like a ghost!" he'd say. I would have preferred to be a ghost, but instead, I felt more like a fixture in the house, something like a throw pillow on the couch, not making a sound but absorbing theirs.

Once again, nothing in my life was sustainable. One evening I got home after curfew and Diane made it known that my presence in their house was a burden. While I'm sure having some random girl who used to play Oregon Trail in your computer class sleeping on your couch for a year and a half isn't the best thing in the world, I'd hardly call it a burden. But then again, we are all encumbered in different ways. I had to get admitted to college, graduate, and find a job that provided financial stability not only for me but also for my family. I also had to bring my brother back to the United States so he could have the same opportunities I did and maybe even eventually help me carry some of the burdens. And Diane was burdened by her daughter's love life because Diane was married to a man who was convinced God didn't approve of homosexuality. If I were Diane, I thought, I'd feel more embarrassed than burdened, but that was my coping mechanism at work: harsh comebacks (even if only said in my head) to try to lessen the blow, to cover up the fact that I was hurt by her statement that I was indeed a burden.

In a weird attempt to please the woman who was my savior in a lot of ways, I wouldn't get back to their house late again. I couldn't risk messing it all up. So instead of running to my uncle's or over to Merva's, I ran back to the shelves of Disney movies to cope. One afternoon I was watching *Mulan,* timing it so that when Diane got home, the movie would be over and I would be at the table, doing my homework like the good little rule follower that I was. When the front door opened as Mulan willed her way to the top of the post to retrieve the arrow while the other soldiers slept, I expected to hear Stacy stroll down the hallway to her room, but instead Diane walked in. She said snarkily, "Oh, so your homework is already done?"

I replied, "Hi, Diane," and hoped she wouldn't push the issue. She questioned me again, more directly. Remembering my mother's words—*Elizabeth, en alguien tiene que caber la prudencia*—I replied calmly, "I will get my work done. Don't worry, Diane."

I watched as Diane crossed her arms in disapproval. "No more movies if your homework isn't done," she snapped. "Turn it off and get going." She gestured to the remote.

Without thinking, I bit back. "I think I know how to manage

my own time, Diane," I said through clenched teeth. "And I do it quite well." While the thinning thread of prudence kept me from sarcastically asking her if Stacy got straight As, a stream of curse words ran through my head. *Vieja metiche,* I thought to myself.

Diane stood in silence with pursed lips, shocked that I'd talked back to her. Without another word, she turned on her heels and walked down the hallway toward her room. Once I heard the door slam, I unpaused the movie and kept watching. I was only a year and a half away from graduating, I reminded myself. I still had the number one ranking on my transcript. I slept on a couch for my education. I left my family for my education. I owned nothing but my education. I could let go of the fact that Diane neglected me, but I wouldn't let her interfere with the way that I got things done.

In the days that followed, Diane gave me the silent treatment. For the first time since moving in with them, I wasn't worried about minimizing myself to make her life easier. I wasn't a carnival fish that she could keep in a little glass bowl. Even if I had to leave, I knew that I'd be able to figure something out. For the first time in a long time, I had confidence in my ability to move forward. As always, I found a solution.

A few days later, I handed the house keys back to Diane, grateful to have survived in a place that took so much out of me. *I'm not your burden anymore,* I thought to myself as I walked out of their home.

18

SPEAKING FOR CHANGE

Without my parents or brother in it, el cuartito felt spacious and empty. The bunk beds had been removed, and only the queen bed, which felt massive compared to a couch, remained. The last time I was here, my dad assured us all that it was temporary, but this time it was the closest thing to permanent I'd had since my parents' visas got denied. This room once represented all our family had lost, but now the glorified shed beside my tío's trailer represented everything I had and everything I had left to gain.

I felt my lungs expand as I sprawled across the bed. Whiskey stretched out on the cool gray concrete floor below. For as long as I could remember, I had feasted on arbitrary milestones and accomplishments; much of my solace had always been placed in the future.

La próxima vez que vea a mis papas . . .

I'll bring my brother back in a few more years . . .

Cuando me gradúe de la universidad . . .
Financial freedom is waiting after college . . .
Algún día seré libre . . .

But being back in el cuartito—off the Hernandezes' couch and away from their micromanaging and dysfunctional noise—I enjoyed a silence I hadn't experienced in years. A silence so nourishing that even the roar of the train passing a few feet away from my room couldn't intrude on it. *My room*—the words felt foreign and welcome. I was with my family again. Family who wouldn't be burdened by me or kick me out. Family who would feed me, whose food tasted like home; whose language sounded like home.

For the first time in a long time, I reminded myself that my parents didn't abandon me. I could breathe, and I could simply be. This felt foreign and yet welcome.

———————

Not long after moving back into el cuartito, I left for a four-day trip to Washington, D.C., with the Jewish-Latino Teen Coalition of Southern Arizona. I had been selected to be a member of JLTC after an intense application and interview process the previous fall, and the trip was a culmination of our time together. As a group of multi-gendered, multiethnic students from different high schools and socioeconomic classes, we had spent months together in weekly workshops centered on cultural awareness and political advocacy. Along with getting to know one another, we also selected a policy issue that was compelling to us to study and lobby for in D.C. Despite my passionate advocacy for immigration to be our political issue of choice, our group ultimately decided on gun control. Since the shooting at Safeway in which Representative Gabby Giffords had been injured had happened only a few years ago, it was an issue that was getting a lot of airtime in our community. To the others, anti-immigration laws were more of a slow death when compared to bullets.

Despite our different experiences and social classes, I felt incredibly close with the other students in JLTC. It was the first time in my life that I was friends with wealthy kids, often going to their giant houses for meetings and staying longer to hang out and swim in their pools. Before JLTC, I didn't know that wealthy people could care about political issues in the same way that I did, especially when certain policies didn't impact them directly. But I quickly learned that Jewish communities had long responded powerfully to human rights issues, holding to the principles of Martin Luther King Jr., when he said, "Injustice anywhere is a threat to justice everywhere." Jewish communities knew the impact of racial segregation and hatred and were committed to being a part of eradicating it across ethnicities.

JLTC was also my first exposure to how people from different backgrounds could unite and work together for change. And even though the political issue chosen was gun control, the group still made room to learn about the impact of anti-immigration laws on the Latino community. For one of the first times, I felt respected. All the Latinos in the group were moved that the Jewish kids were genuinely concerned about and connected to our humanity and the humanity of the people who mowed their nice lawns and trimmed their secure hedges. We started off as a group of Latino and Jewish kids who didn't know one another, and over time we bonded over the possibility of progress, equality, and equity.

———————

As I rolled my suitcase full of blazers from thrift shops and slacks from sale racks across the Tucson airport, I felt nauseous as conflicting emotions tried to coexist. The suitcase that had come with me across the border, that I had lived out of while I slept on couches, was now being used in a trip to the nation's capital. The capital where lawmakers meet and laws are passed—the same laws that rejected my parents' visa application, that fractured our family, that put me, a sixteen-year-old girl, in the unenviable position of choosing future over family. At the same time, I couldn't deny the childlike excitement I felt about traveling, about seeing more of the United States, about being in a new city with new people, alongside friends. And not only to hang out, but to learn, to lobby, to use our presence and our knowledge for good. This was my version of a high school party, my version of a good time.

The stated goals of the trip were that we employ our advocacy skills in meetings with representatives and play a role in helping push the needle toward change. But for me, it was so much more than that. As we walked the streets of D.C. and up the stairs of the U.S. Capitol, I saw a world beyond my own. Everywhere we went, people walked with purpose. I saw people of races I'd never personally encountered before. I saw restaurants with cuisines I'd never tried, with entrées I'd never heard of. This trip was more than educational, it was about exposure—to processes, people, and energy. All of it fanned the flame of my fire, my drive to succeed, to impact and enact change. The whole experience reassured me that I wasn't alone, that there were buildings and cities full of people with the same fire.

One of those buildings housed the Religious Action Center (RAC), a hub of Jewish social justice. The Washington office is a short walk from the White House's front lawn. On the day that we were set to spend time at the Religious Action Center, they were holding a pre-immigration-rally conference. Rabbis, clergypeople, and other activists made up the one hundred plus people in attendance. It felt serendipitous that we would be there on that specific day. As different people spoke about the issues of immigration and anti-immigration laws, as they talked about time and funds being given to fight this urgent fight, I felt an overwhelming sense of community, of support and belonging. And if I'm being honest, it was a feeling I had never ever felt with my family when it came to fighting the systemic issues of immigration. This wasn't their fault—I was learning that it was one of the many ways the system beats people down so they're too busy simply surviving to have time to fight for change.

I was feverishly taking notes when one of our JLTC leaders, Lew Hamburger, leaned in and asked me if I'd like to speak, to tell my story of how immigration laws have affected my family. Before I had any time to feel nervous or think through what I would even say, I said yes. I had never been afraid of public speaking; I knew how to get and keep people's attention and interest. I could sound confident even if I didn't feel it. After all, I was my mother's daughter, so I knew how to present myself.

With hundreds of eyes on me, I told my story:

I was born into a family of hardworking immigrants in a city only an hour away from the U.S.–Mexico border. Worried about the quality of education in the low-income neighborhood that we lived in, my parents toured schools until they found one that satisfied their expectations. Like many immigrants, they dreamt of a life full of opportunity for me and my younger brother, making our education their priority. I knew from my father's dust-covered hands and my mother's warm and tired smile that nothing would make them happier than to see us succeed. On the first day of kindergarten, I remember how she held my hand. I remember how, before she kissed me goodbye, my mother whispered into my ear, "Tienes que ser la mejor," you have to be the best.

When I was fifteen years old, my parents' visas expired. Confident that it would be an easy renewal and that the process would allow them to come back to the United States, my parents left me with my younger brother for what should have been only a short time. However, a week turned into a month, and that month has turned into years.

My parents' visas were denied not once, but twice—a thought I had never considered. I never thought that my smart and amazing eight-year-old brother would not be able to finish his school year or that I would never get to enjoy my mother's comforting enchiladas after a soccer game. I was thrown into a reality I didn't want as my brother left everything behind: his school, his friends, and his life. He crossed borders indefinitely to join our parents in a different country.

But the thought that I might have to leave this country, my country, a country that many believed that I did not belong in, was one that I couldn't bear.

I've spent the last year learning how to adapt quickly and prudently in different environments. My school, concerned about my well-being, has enrolled me in a dropout prevention program for homeless youth, tiptoeing around me as if I could break at any moment. Which if I had time to break down, that might actually be the case.

I've been encouraged to go back to my family.

I've been told that my life would be better if I went back to Mexico.

I understand why my situation is treated with such caution. Among second-generation immigrants of Hispanic descent, only about 20 percent ever make it to post-secondary school, and only half of those between the ages of twenty-five and thirty-five have a high school diploma. In addition, the Pew Hispanic Center estimates that there are more than 4 million U.S.-born children of undocumented parents, thousands of whom are facing the consequences of family separation due to the broken immigration law.

Here I am without my parents, considered homeless, and it is a direct result of Congress's refusal to engage in immigration reform. All these factors have increased my chances of dropping out by 87 percent.

But those statistics fail to take into account the extreme sacrifices made by immigrant families like mine. They erase my parents' resisting their decision to let me stay, unsure of my future, and how they felt when they held my younger brother as he crumbled and watched me wave goodbye to him from the other side of steel gates.

I am one of many who have feared and anticipated the separation of their family for their whole lives. But for the love of my family, I have pushed forward. Stubbornly I've ignored the advice to take easier classes and lower my horizons. Instead, I have found support in teachers who encouraged me while refusing to coddle me. I have sought out programs that value the talent and skills of kids at low-income Arizona school districts. I've applied for programs like the Jewish-Latino Teen Coalition, which has brought me to D.C. this week to put our advocacy and lobbying skills to work. And with one year left before I graduate, I sit at the top of my class.

Still, I am resentful that my hardworking parents aren't here in the States, supporting and raising me. I am resentful that my brother, an American citizen, had to readjust to a Spanish-speaking school, and that at such a young age, he is losing the English language and is forfeiting the bilingualism that I enjoy.

The politics behind immigration—the gridlock, the lack of reform, and the unfulfilled promises—have led to the raids and targeted deportation and separation of thousands of nonthreatening immigrant families. We cannot afford to be submissive. We cannot let people, human beings, face disadvantages simply because they are subject to unconscious biases and misconceptions.

Instead, we must whisper into the ears of all our children as they run into their first day of school, encouraging them to be the best in a country that flourishes when different voices come together. We must remind them, and remind ourselves, of the power in our voices and the potential that we hold.

This system is broken, and we must find every opportunity to make sure that America knows that people like me, from families like mine, belong here.

Applause erupted, echoing off the walls. At the next break, I was approached by countless people who thanked me and assured me that I had a voice and a place not only in the country, but in the Capitol. I relished in the attention and affirmation. It made me feel like my story mattered; what I had been through, what I was still going through, mattered. When I spoke, people listened. It was a power I had never felt before. Before, my education held power, but now I had power. My words—my story—had power.

We walked outside into the fresh spring air of D.C. and Lew leaned in again. "How does it feel to have told your story in the same building where Martin Luther King Jr. joined others to draft the Civil Rights Act of 1964?" he asked. The dark hair on my Brown skin rose as if to proclaim that I mattered. *I matter.* I spoke in the same room he spoke. I took notes in the same room he drafted an act that would in turn help crack open the door to immigrants, to my family, to me.

I spent the rest of the trip immersed in the energy of D.C. as I contemplated how I would help open the door even further, even if only by an inch. How I would not just invite people to see us immigrants as human, but *demand* that they do so? I made another choice about my major, deciding in that moment to be a lobbyist. I had tasted an ounce of the sweat and tears of the career and I was addicted.

The day we got back to Tucson, mere hours after speaking in the iconic Religious Action Center, I was back in the kitchen at KFC, working the closing shift. Anytime I closed, I'd put extra chicken that I knew wouldn't sell in the fryer toward the end of the night. Chicken that I could pack up and take to my tío Miguel's apartment. Miguel was in Mexico, waiting on the verdict of his visa renewal while my tía Rocio and cousins stayed behind in the United States. I knew what it was like to stay behind. I knew what it was like to be hungry.

So I did what my dad and I would do when we'd sneak into movies without paying. I stole a little bit back.

19

HELLO, YES, I'M ALLERGIC TO FAILURE

When I was a kid, whenever we drove by the University of Arizona, I'd eagerly point toward the redbrick buildings with the floor-to-ceiling windows. "I want to be an architect," I'd say from the back seat.

Glancing at me in the rearview mirror, my dad would smile. "Claro, mija, I'm sure there's a scholarship for that if you work hard enough."

Then after a field trip to watch the orchestra, I'd come home and inform my parents of my new dream. "I want to be a performer," I'd explain. "I can sing and act and play instruments." My dreams and desires changed depending on the day and my mood. I simply wanted to do it all, and my parents never shied away from letting me know that there would be a path for me. "When there is a will, there is a way," they'd say. In a world full of noes, my parents always said yes.

A decade later, as I started the college application process,

I went back to the memories of my parents' unfettered encouragement. Despite the high tuition and the low acceptance numbers, I knew that there was a way toward the school of my dreams. By then I was used to looking for opportunities and asking for help. I'd found scholarships that helped improve my state-funded high school experience. One summer, a scholarship allowed me to attend a Young Democrats of America conference in Texas. Another scholarship earned me a free trip to Brazil with National Geographic. Time and time again I found myself in situations of my own making, standing out as the only Spanish speaker or as the quirky kid with the borrowed hiking backpack. Poverty teaches you a resourcefulness you never need to learn if you are nurtured in privilege.

Hoping to be citizens one day or at least to get their visas renewed, my parents couldn't afford to draw attention to our family, even if it would have helped us get ahead. We never got food stamps. We avoided government programs. By forgoing welfare that we qualified for, my parents kept themselves under the radar. With them now in Mexico, I learned to capitalize on my situation. If I was ever going to get into college, to have a chance at succeeding, I needed to stand out, even if I was standing out because I was poor.

At school, I was one of maybe a few students that truly stressed about getting into college. For the most part, my classmates were content with attending the local community college or the University of Arizona.

"I don't understand why you're trying so hard on these applications," my classmate Casey said. "U of A is cheaper anyways."

"If I somehow manage to get into schools outside of Arizona,

I shouldn't have to pay that much," I replied. "There's financial aid."

"Good luck with that, though you might have a chance since you're Mexican," she snipped, insinuating that I'd get in only thanks to my diversity checkbox. I ignored her and the other voices who told me that what I wanted wasn't possible. I applied to more than twenty schools: Columbia, Middlebury, Williams, Georgetown, Penn. I was forced to stop only after I ran out of application fee waivers. At the same time, I'd sabotage myself when it came to my applications to the big schools, either applying late or submitting incomplete documentation so that I wouldn't be disappointed when the rejection letters came. It was easier to blame my lack of timeliness rather than my lack of worthiness. I'd worked my ass off to be the best, and life had still taught me to expect the worst.

I applied the same principle to college applications, spending hours and hours writing nonstop, perfecting my personal statements, and tailoring my essays and dreams to each school. At Georgetown, I could pursue politics; at Duke, I could pursue environmental studies. On January 1, the last day for submissions, I finally felt relieved. There was nothing more I could do.

But relief was an unfamiliar feeling, so I quickly fell back to my emotional wheelhouse of anxiety. There was nothing more I could do. *Oh my god, there is nothing more I can do.* I had to wait. And for what? For someone else to look over my papers and decide my future. For someone else to look over every applicant's papers and decide who was worthy of being accepted. Suddenly the process of applying to college was too similar to my parents applying for their visas.

For weeks and months, I sat in limbo. I thought of my dad sitting in government offices, probably sweating as they questioned him. I thought of my mom, staying on top of attorneys to ensure they did their job so she could get back to the United States. I thought of my brother, wailing on the other side of the border, watching me walk away. There has never been security in limbo.

Meanwhile, my friends joked about how waiting on admission letters felt like being left on read by the guy you like. Sure, if the guy you liked was an Ivy League school. I occupied two worlds—the world of a normal teenager in the final semester of her senior year, and the world of a first-generation Brown girl living in the country that supposedly is her home by birth, while her parents remain rejected at the border. The world that could joke about admission letters being love letters and the world with a future that hinged on the contents of each piece of mail addressed to Elizabeth Camarillo Gutierrez.

The first letter arrived on a random Tuesday—jammed into the mailbox because of its size. As I reached for it, my stomach twisted into a knot of fear and excitement. Big letters were a good sign. NYU was stamped across it in big purple type. Somehow I managed to not tear it open right then and there. Instead, I ran inside and sat on my bed in el cuartito, with Whiskey lolling at my feet and anxiety pounding in my chest. The small room filled with every doubt I'd ever had about college and my worth. *I'm coming from a shitty public school. My SAT score is good only at my school, nowhere else.* I tore open the envelope. *I haven't created a company like the kids I read about on the college forums. There's no chance of nepotism because my name holds no weight.* I slid out the letter. *I was not the perfect well-rounded student. It's an uneven playing field, but it doesn't matter that it's uneven—all that matters is that I am not even on the field.* "Dear Elizabeth." *Why did I even apply to these places? I have set myself up for disappointment, failure, and rejection.* "On behalf of the admissions committee, it is my honor and privilege to share with you that you have been admitted . . ."

I read those words over and over again, desperate to assure myself that I was reading them correctly, that my eyes weren't playing a cruel joke. ". . . you have been admitted . . ." *Oh my god, I did it. I did it. I'm getting out of Arizona and I'm going to NYU!* The relief rolled down my spine, taking a weight I'd carried for most of my life with it.

I did it.

I skimmed through the rest of the packet, reading only enough to know that the financial aid packet was shit. Still, I called my dad.

"Papa, I got into NYU!" I screamed. "New York University."

"Felicidades, mija," he chirped. "I knew you had nothing to worry about."

"What about the money?" I asked. "This letter says I'll have to pay twenty thousand a year."

"Scholarships and loans, mija," he assured me. "Whatever it takes is worth it . . . an education? That is priceless."

The next letter arrived from Williams College, one of the top liberal arts schools in the nation and a school with only a 15 percent acceptance rate. A school often referred to as a Little Ivy.

Dear Elizabeth,

On behalf of all of us here at Williams, I am delighted to offer you admission to the class of 2018! Congratulations!

Oh my god, I got into Williams. I was euphoric.

The next letter arrived, my first from an Ivy League school.

Dear Elizabeth,

    Congratulations!

Holy fuck. I got into Cornell.

Columbia: accepted.

Duke: accepted.

Georgetown: accepted.

Amherst: accepted.

Duke: accepted.

Yale: rejected. Fuck them anyway.

Penn: accepted.

As letters rolled in, my shock grew. I couldn't believe it. I had gone from thinking I was not going to get in anywhere, to praying that I'd at least get in somewhere out of state, to acceptance after acceptance. (Except Yale, but I'm over that. Totally over it. Probably don't even need to mention it.)

Harvard arrived, and I anticipated a rejection since I had turned in my application late after running out of fee waivers.

Dear Elizabeth,

    I am writing to inform you that the Committee on Admissions cannot at this time make a final decision on your application for a place in next year's entering class. However, because of your achievements and promise, the Committee has voted to place your name on a waiting list shall a place become available later.

I was so pissed off at myself. If only I had turned it in on time, I would've gotten in. I *know* I would've gotten in. The best part about Harvard was that my parents were aware of its prestige. The school's name was recognizable regardless of which side of the river or border you found yourself on. They would've had bragging rights in any and every town they stepped foot in. My acceptance into college had always been as much about my parents as it had been about me. For them, it was validation that their sacrifices were worth it; that their choices were the right ones.

For me, it was validation that *I* was worth it.

In so many ways, getting into college was my end game. I knew that at some point in high school a lot of us convince ourselves that it's the absolute worst time in our life, and once we graduate, it'll get better. I wasn't that naive. It was simply that throughout high school, I'd had such real-world adult problems that I felt as though maybe I had reached my quota of trauma or stress. I would no longer have to prove myself. I would no longer have to look over my shoulder to see who was coming up to take my number one ranking on the transcript or my seat in a college's entering freshman class. I had done the work; I had been accepted. Now I could live life. Now I could be happy. Now I could be proud . . . of myself and my parents.

And yet as soon as pride crept in, as soon as happiness crept in, I also felt sadness and self-doubt. At school, I immediately started downplaying my acceptance into these prestigious schools. When a teacher would find out and congratulate me, I'd respond with a joke about how affirmative action was the only reason I got accepted. In some ways, I wanted them to assure me that I got it because I worked hard, because I was smart and capable. It's crazy that even when you sacrifice so much, when you work so hard for a goal and then you reach it, you are met with critics—and for me, the most stringent critic was the one inside my head. But then again, that's what this country does, what white supremacy does to families of immigrants. Families work so hard and sacrifice so much to come here for "a better life" and then are immediately criticized, ridiculed, racially profiled, and eventually turned away by people who have never walked in their shoes. Even as a citizen, I had internalized the immigrant stereotypes of this country—the ones that dehumanize us as monsters or marvel at us as exceptional. Maybe that's why my mom's words were always "you have to be the best." She knew there was no escaping the dehumanization, so she wanted to ensure I was at least marveled at, and a Brown girl from my side of the river getting accepted into three Ivy Leagues and many other private colleges was sure as hell something to marvel at.

Twelve years after my mom told me that I had to be the best, I'd done it. By the end of the school year, I'd pulled off near-perfect grades, even after almost taking down my chemistry classmates with poisonous gas. All around me, people congratulated me. Mr. Becker told me that he was proud. Moved by what I'd gone through, the principal of my school patted me on the back and congratulated me for becoming valedictorian. And still, *I* struggled to feel proud.

"My parents won't be at graduation," I told the principal,

holding back tears. "They won't see what I've accomplished." We came up with a plan.

"We'll make sure to have a live stream running for them to see," he promised. All I wanted was for my parents to witness the return for their sacrifices. I wanted them to know that I had done it.

"If there's a will, there's a way," they'd told me. Somehow I'd found my way.

A month later, on a cool spring night in May, I graduated from high school at the top of my class and took a selfie from the podium with everyone in attendance. Somewhere in the crowd stood my tío Gabriel and my tía Denia, screaming wildly alongside Fernando, whom my grandparents had driven up for the occasion. Though they were hundreds of miles away, I knew that my parents were tuned in. After my speech, I walked off the stage and found my little brother. Hugging him made me feel like I was finally home.

PART THREE

20

WHERE ARE YOU FROM?

It didn't matter that it was August in Arizona or that it would be a humid ninety degrees when I landed in Philadelphia—I had to wear my flannel long-sleeve shirt, heavy jacket, and vintage dark brown Timberland boots on my flight. They were the heaviest things I owned, and I didn't want them to take up room in my suitcases. After months of saving, I could afford only two checked bags. *Not* two overweight checked bags. With a bunch of the travel compression containers they advertised on TV, I squeezed everything I could fit into my two obnoxiously bright suitcases, which were way too big for me to lug on my own. So I did what any resourceful first-gen kid would do . . . I lugged them on my own.

I barely thought about my family on my flight to Philly. As our plane crossed the country, I slowly began to feel freer—away from the shackles I often felt living in Arizona, where I always had to ask for help in order to get around or do the things I loved to do. Now the world was at my fingertips. I read a book the school had assigned to all the freshmen and looked out over the countryside as we cut through the different types of clouds my brother had once told me about. When we landed, I waited with a group of people, some wearing Penn shirts and hats, in the baggage claim area. When my suitcases came around, I awkwardly lifted them off the carousel—grabbing the orange one first and letting the red one go for one more loop around while I regained my composure and strength. Then I lugged the suitcases out of the Philly airport before getting a $10 van share that would take me to my new life at the University of Pennsylvania.

The van driver lifted my suitcases into the trunk (thankfully), and as we started down Route 291, he asked, "Where are you from?" In hindsight, he could've been asking because I was dressed as if I'd come from the snowy mountains of Colorado, but I quickly wrestled, as I always did, with which answer to give. Arizona? Mexico?

"Tucson," I replied, hoping the driver knew how close the city was to Mexico.

"Never heard of it," he replied as he stared forward.

Even though I didn't need a reminder—my assuredness and excitement were at an all-time high—driving through Philly showed me exactly why I'd chosen UPenn. The city was so beautiful and historic; it felt like a place where scholars would live. I was able to visit a lot of the colleges that I was accepted to through admitted-student fly-in programs that were free if your family's income was low enough. I always qualified. Before visiting campuses, I was convinced that I would go to Columbia. According to the holy grail that is *US News and World Report*, Columbia was the highest-ranked school that I'd been accepted to. I felt like it was a given that if I got into the best school, then I would *go* to the best school and live in the best city in the world. New York City was easy to romanticize. The best is always easy to romanticize.

I'd spent the entire month of April of my senior year flying around the country visiting schools. On campus, the guides showed you everything they had to offer, trying to woo you into choosing them. I had high expectations for Columbia, and while it felt like a cool school and I met amazing people there, New York City overwhelmed me. It felt dirty, loud, and fast. While the campus was beautiful, the backdrop of the chaotic city made community feel impossible.

I visited other schools, such as NYU and Macalester, but the moment I stepped onto Penn's cobblestone campus, I thought, *Wow. This feels like college. This feels like education.* I made my way down Locust Walk through the campus, passing a mid-century Victorian Gothic mansion (aka a frat commonly known as Castle) and the green Gothic College Hall. Penn's architecture was striking in its resilience and wisdom—the frat boys being the only downfall, but they're dumb everywhere. Even the ground had history. Quotes from Benjamin Franklin were engraved into the steps, inspiring me with each step I took. The architecture of Penn was imposing and beautiful, almost like how church buildings are big and grandiose to usher you into faith. Penn's campus shocked me into idealistic belief.

Then there were the freshman dorms and the Fisher Fine Arts Library, which made me feel like I was at Hogwarts. As I stared at the long tables in the library, the ones that invite hours of studying, I thought of my dad and me sneaking into Harry Potter movies. In some ways, I felt as though I was sneaking into Penn, too, as if I didn't belong there, as if the full-ride scholarship I'd been offered was more of a charity case than earned, as if I was just a checkmark on their diversity quota initiative. And in other ways, my heart felt calm and invigorated by the atmosphere, as if this could really be home. As always, I straddled many worlds, and there was always tension between them.

When I visited in April, everything was in bloom, and the tall trees arched over Locust Walk with vibrant new life. It was as if nature was also putting on her best show, begging the admitted students to choose the beauty of this place. Students were out picnicking, reading, and sunbathing, and everyone was friendly. In so many ways, they felt like my people. The best of the best, the smartest, the focused, the driven, the welcoming. And Penn could offer what other places didn't: La Casa Latina, a cultural center in the middle of campus run by an old Puerto Rican man named Johnny. Being around Johnny felt as comfortable as the leather couches that the Latino kids stretched out on. He evoked home, and his entire purpose was to help us make the transition and thrive at Penn.

During my first tour of the campus, one of our stops was stocked with posters that stated *At Penn I Will . . .* People could take one, fill in the blank, pose for a photo, and then pin it up. Without hesitation or second-guessing myself, I wrote: *At Penn I Will Change the World.* Like the people I sat beside in Catholic mass, I genuinely believed it. I had faith. That's what Penn does. Penn is an architectural wonder, old and new and filled with history. It made me feel invincible and focused: I was there to learn, to make the most out of this institution where everything was at my fingertips. I felt like I could go there now so I could change the world later.

Despite knowing what I felt deep down, I was torn when it came to making the final decision of where I would go. With a couple of days left before Decision Day, I had narrowed it down to Columbia and Penn. While Columbia felt stale compared to the vibrant campus of Penn and the city of Philadelphia, my parents knew about Columbia. They were familiar with its reputation of excellence, while they didn't know much about Penn and kept confusing it with Penn State. I couldn't bear the thought of getting into a private Ivy League university and having it be confused with a public state school. Even as someone who came from nothing, I was still acting a little elitist.

At the end of Mr. Golden's class one day, he asked if I had made my decision. I told him that I hadn't, but that I *had* made a Venn diagram and that I was probably going to make a spreadsheet next.

"Elizabeth, flip a coin," he said. *What?! He wants me to make the most important decision of my entire life by flipping a fucking coin?*

"When it's up in the air, you're going to know at that moment what you want it to land on. If it lands on one side and you get a gut instinct wishing it had landed on the other, then you're going to know the answer."

In other words, Mr. Golden was encouraging me to listen to my heart—a response foreign to me. Indeed, this response is foreign to a lot of people whose families are poor or are immigrants, or in my case, both. It is a privilege to be able to listen to your heart.

And regarding this decision, it was a privilege I had.

I dug in the bottom of my backpack for a penny, and without referencing my Venn diagram or my as-yet-to-be-executed spreadsheet, I flipped the coin. I couldn't tell you what it landed on, but as it flipped end over end through the air, I knew the answer—the side I wanted it to land on.

"It's Penn."

Penn was old and wise, a place where I could absorb everything and be a scholar. I could see myself there, and as much as I viewed feelings as distractions, I could *feel* myself there, too. Philly was the city of brotherly love, and no matter how much I had romanticized the reputation of New York and Columbia, I wanted a place where I could make friends who felt like family, build a community, and a home. It wasn't as high as Columbia in the *US News and World Report* rankings, but for the first time in my life, I got to value the concept of home more than I valued ranking in my education.

When the van share approached the campus, the road ahead of us suddenly closed. I guess it was normal for there to be closures around campus on move-in day. The driver pulled over, put on his hazard lights, and hurriedly grabbed my giant suitcases out of the back. After a kind "Good luck," he hopped back in the driver's seat, executed a U-turn, and drove off. I stood on the sidewalk with my backpack strapped on my back, the bright orange and red suitcases at my feet. With a deep breath and a mental note to relax my shoulders, I attempted to walk to my assigned dorm while pulling both suitcases simultaneously. Within a few steps it became evident that this was going to be impossible. I could have fit inside my suitcases; they were quite literally bigger than I was. I couldn't believe I had overcome everything I had only to finally get to Penn, *my* Ivy League school, and be completely overwhelmed by my heavy-ass suitcases.

From a distance, I watched parents help their kids unload their bags into the dorms at the Quad. I was too far away and they were too distracted to see the lone incoming freshman down the street struggling along. Instead, I resorted to the only option I had left. Using both hands, I grabbed the orange suitcase first, pulled it fifteen feet toward campus. Then I walked fifteen feet back to the red one, grabbed it, and wheeled it toward the orange one. Orange one, fifteen more feet; back to the red one; etc. It was like a scene from a movie that was a comedy . . . and a tragedy.

Dripping in sweat from my heavy clothing, I finally got to the entrance of the campus, and a guy came running toward me. Javier introduced himself and seemed immediately to know what my situation was. He insisted on helping me carry my luggage the final blocks to my dorm.

"Where are you from?" he asked. I didn't hesitate to tell him that I'm from both Arizona and Mexico. Javier was Mexican and said he was also a first-gen student, but I already knew that. When you're from a family of immigrants or come from poverty, you have a sixth sense for finding others like you, for knowing who you can trust and with what information. There's an approachable energy or vibe we give off. Or maybe it was different from the vibes of Tiffany Trump or the kids of Russian oligarchs who were also roaming around campus. Regardless, Javier was the first person I met on my first day at Penn, and his presence reminded me that I would find myself there, that there would be people like me, that I had made the right choice.

I remembered a story Dad used to tell me about when he was a kid and visited England. He was amazed by the age of everything there, telling me, "Todo está viejo, pero está bien hecho. Everything is old, but it's well-built." As Javier and I walked past the buildings that had drawn me in—with their history and sturdiness—I was reminded of my dad's observations, and I knew that like the buildings themselves, my education was going to last.

21

CHOSEN FAMILY

My roommate Cindy and her parents were already in our shared dorm room by the time Javier dropped me off with a big smile and a "buena suerte." Before moving in, Cindy and I had messaged back and forth a few times after we'd been matched.

"Just so you know, I'm super gassy. Thought I would get that out sooner rather than later," I warned.

"LOL. I burp a lot, so same," she replied.

Over a string of texts, we got to know each other quite well—including our mutual love-hate relationship with KFC and our responsibilities as the oldest daughter in an immigrant household.

"We deserve a reward," Cindy said.

"No, but actually—this is exhausting," I agreed.

Cindy and her parents were quiet but extremely nice and helpful, speaking to one another in an easy flow of English and

Vietnamese as they moved in her things. When Cindy's mom and dad were about to leave, I hugged them because that's what I do when I say goodbye. Awkwardly they smiled and said, "Good luck," as they turned to Cindy to tell her they loved her and had left the mini fridge full of stuffed Tupperware and snacks. When I turned around, Cindy was laughing.

"My parents don't even hug *me*," she said. "But don't worry, that was cute." I smiled, wondering when I'd next get to see and hug my own parents.

I watched Cindy set up her bed immaculately. She had a full comforter set that matched her pillowcases. On the wall, she hung strings with pictures attached by mini clothespins. I, on the other hand, didn't have sheets or a towel or even shampoo. Hey, I was practicing minimalism before it was cool. Still, I definitely needed some essentials, so I quickly checked Google Maps and found the nearest Walmart was only an hour-and-a-half walk away. To me, that felt pretty short, and it was also a good way to see the city. When I asked Cindy, who was born and raised in Philly, if she wanted to go with me, she stared.

"You want to *walk* there?" she asked. "That's across the city!"

I was used to riding my bike across Tucson between suburbs. "I mean, I'd rather pay for a cab on the way back than on the way there," I replied.

Cindy stared at me for a while before replying. "True," she finally said. "Yeah, I'll come."

I don't remember the specific questions on the roommate questionnaire, but I'm pretty sure Penn didn't ask "Are you the oldest daughter of immigrants? Do you come from a poor family?" But Cindy and I got matched as roommates, and if they had asked that, we both would have checked yes. When we finally got back from Walmart hours later, we both confessed.

"You're poor, too, aren't you?" I asked.

"Yes, thank god we got put together," she replied. To know that there would be at least one person on campus who was like me gave me a sense of relief.

Cindy and I threw ourselves into the next few weeks of New Student Orientation activities. Although I'd always been quiet and focused on school, something came out of me when I first got to Penn that made me excited about meeting *everyone*.

"You're such a social butterfly," Cindy would say, laughing as I waved at people I'd known for less than a day. I don't know where my excitement came from. Maybe it was because we lived in the Quad, the best freshman dorms, where they'd filmed part of *Transformers*. Sure, STDs were rampant and there were bathrooms trashed by drunk freshmen, but this shit show was in an architectural marvel with Gothic-looking mini libraries, spiraling staircases, and beautiful hardwood floors. Our section of the Quad was called Riepe House; it was the baby dorm, whose unofficial motto was "good food, good company." Riepe's live-in faculty hosted cookie nights every Wednesday, where I found myself drifting around the room, introducing myself, talking with anyone and everyone, while Cindy snagged as many free cookies as possible. Then there was the Sunday coffee open house, which was hosted by Professor Ralph Rosen and his wife Ellen. They were really into coffee, and Ralph even roasted his own beans. They always had fresh orange juice and tons of snacks from Trader Joe's. I quickly took to the Rosens and made them my Penn parents.

You hear of the "Ivy League spirit," of faculty in residence and the integration of intellectualism into your everyday life, including your social life, but I never expected it to be real. I thought it was just a savvy marketing tool for luring in the super smart kids with big egos who thought they were better than the average person. In other words, I thought it was a savvy marketing tool used to lure kids like me. And maybe it *was* part of the marketing, but it was also part of the culture.

I had never been in lecture halls and classrooms like the ones at Penn—unfussy boring rooms filled with lively, stimulating discussions. I could have conversations here with students unlike any I had ever had in my high school classrooms. Conversations about philosophy and politics and globalization and sustainability. It didn't really matter to me that a lot of the kids came from wealthier, more privileged backgrounds. Of course I knew that there were people with a lot of money, but I was naive about exactly how wealthy people were. All I knew was that even though I had nothing, at Penn, we had everything and we could do *anything*. In my mind, we had all made it here somehow and the playing field had been leveled. Well, except for in my Scandalous Arts class, which I signed up for thinking it would combine my love of art and gossip. As we studied the poetry of Catullus, I realized it had never occurred to me that a sparrow could be anything but a literal bird, let alone a metaphor for a penis. Maybe they taught that kind of stuff in private schools, but in Tucson's public schools, they were busy wiping out ethnic studies, so penis poems didn't stand a chance.

During my first semester, I attended bio classes and writing classes and waited for the gotcha moments to happen. At Penn, we were all the best, and for a while I didn't feel like I needed to compete. In a lot of ways, the pressure was initially tamped down. I had access to food, shelter, learning, and community. It had been years since I'd had all my basic needs met in a way that allowed me to relax, that allowed me to socialize and find community. I knew that it wouldn't always be this way: of course I'd have to keep applying for and earning scholarships, and then I'd need an internship and a job. I knew that in a couple of years, I had to get my brother back to the States.

During phone calls with Fer, I'd remind him what was at stake. "Fer, you're going to love college and school back in America," I promised. "It's just a matter of time before I bring you back with me."

"Cuándo?" he'd ask. "When will I be able to go?"

"We'll figure it out later," I said reassuringly. "But first we'll have to plan a trip for you to visit me!"

My new friends and I weren't just hanging at faculty get-togethers in the dorms. We attended frat parties and went out dancing. It didn't matter that I didn't drink—for a while, no one even knew, so there weren't any strange misperceptions of me that I had to dismantle. Social life was easy and fun, and I had the best of friends. I knew people like Ivan, who was a first-gen student from Georgia studying at Wharton—the business school at Penn that I hadn't yet realized was famous. Ivan and I went to museums and movies. We talked about art and politics. Besides being an incredible person and a friend, Ivan also taught me a lot about what it meant to be queer in this world. Over and over again, I was moved by the vulnerability he shared with me.

My group of friends changed over time. I met people like

Richard and Carol, who were also Mexican. Being around them kept me motivated. Carol was also first generation and worked her ass off to get into and through college. She knew early on that she wanted to be a dentist, and she had the most perfect smile, so her plan made sense. Then there was Richard, who I swear to God was one of the smartest people I met. While I struggled in biology class, Richard napped and got perfect test scores. He worked hard and played hard—a feat I didn't think was possible but admired. I latched on to my friends tightly. It was as if we were all the same people in different fonts. I'm not sure if they realized how much their presence shaped my life. For the first time, I didn't feel lonely. I was not an anomaly or an exception. I found people that I could relate to and have conversations with—people who brought me out of my shell. At some points in high school, I would withdraw from others and go silent, feeling I had nothing to say or there was nothing worthwhile to talk about. In contrast, at Penn, I was a social butterfly, an extrovert, wanting to wring every ounce of nourishment out of my experience.

My friends were the cocreators of some of those beautiful moments. I enjoyed their big smiles and the stupid shit we'd do together, like taking shots of hot sauces at the Mexican restaurant in South Philly or watching *Lady Bird* together and crying in the rain while calling our moms. Or when they all pitched in to buy me a new camera when mine was stolen. We cried together, laughed together, bombed tests together. The time Richard and I rescued Cindy from a party when she complained about wanting to go to sleep. The obnoxious laughter from Zeeshan and Andre at Wawa over 1 A.M. slushies. The moments we gave one another our full attention, our full presence. They were the people who cared about me in ways foreign to me, ways not dependent on achievements or accolades.

My friends quickly became the most important part of my life, my chosen family, offering me the support and home that I craved. But if there's one thing I know about homes and families, it's that eventually they always disappear.

22

CANADA GREY GOOSE

went into my sophomore year only slightly more prepared than I had freshman year. Away from the comfort of the Quad and the familiarity of my shared room with Cindy, I began to feel the pressure that Penn was known to foster. The year before, I'd read articles about Maddie, a freshman at Penn who had died by suicide a year before I'd started school. After finding out about it, I'd scrolled through her still public social media pages, studying the posts of someone who looked like she had it all. Maddie was an athlete, she was pretty, she was smart enough to get into Penn.

She had everything, I thought to myself. *Why would anyone want to die with a life like hers?* Now, my second year in, I started to understand. Penn was described as the social Ivy by many, touting its "work hard, play hard" culture. I'd watch friends and acquaintances all around me get blackout drunk on the weekends, and yet they were the same people who had perfect GPAs. For a while

I played along, pretending to have more fun at BYOs and parties than I actually was. The truth was, I felt like I was on some sort of hamster wheel. My grades flatlined, with Bs and the occasional C. How did the people around me seem to have it all figured out? Were they all hiding their feelings of self-doubt, depression, and emptiness in the same way that I was? In the same way that Maddie had?

At first I didn't tell anyone that I didn't drink. It didn't feel like something I needed to mention. The novelty of going out late at night in a big city like Philadelphia was enough to keep me energized. However, as time passed, I watched my friends hive off into different clubs, fraternities, and sororities. Every club had a process for you to join, even the ones you'd expect to be stupid and low effort. At "screenings" or "interviews," other students assessed you, asking what drink would best describe you. At Penn, having a social life was easier if alcohol was involved. The less you remembered, the more people seemed to like you.

My closest friends caught on to the fact that I didn't drink after a while, asking me if I had a specific reason for not doing it. "Can I ask why?" they'd always start. "Is it your religion?" The never-ending questions felt something like an inquisition. The truth was, I didn't have an answer, at least one that would satisfy them.

"I just don't want to." I'd laugh coyly, hoping everyone's perception of me wouldn't change. In high school, I'd been a straight arrow, following the rules and staying out of trouble. I stayed away from weed and drugs. For the most part, I'd avoided relationships with boys as well, breaking up with my high school "boyfriend" after things started to feel forced and clingy. I didn't want to feel tethered or held back by anything. In college, I felt I didn't need alcohol and drugs. Why should I do something to fit in?

Still, I wanted to be *normal*. And every time somebody offered me a glass, a shot, or a beer, I wanted to say yes. I wanted to take it and let myself go. I wanted to make out with strangers without obsessively wondering if they brushed their teeth, if they had STDs, or if they were secretly Trump supporters. Maybe it would be fun to pass out on the sticky floor of frat houses next to the piles of puffy black jackets that the rich white girls kept losing and asking for in our class's Facebook group the next day. Maybe it would have been easier to forget the fact that I missed my family and that I felt guilty about not calling them. It would have been easier to be numb to the fact that I was missing Fer's milestones. Instead, I stayed sober, watching the chaos unfold around me.

The day after a party, I'd log on to Facebook, the feed filled with classmates looking for items and jackets that they'd lost the night before. Jackets I'd watched them heap in dark sticky hallways.

> Hi sorry to post this but I lost my size S black Canada Goose jacket with no distinguishing features other than it's a black Canada Goose. Might have left at Castle, the frat for rich international kids, last night. Lmk if you've seen it!!!

Sometimes I was so tired at parties that I *almost* felt drunk. After a while, I'd let myself fade into the crowd, smiling and swaying, blending in. My closest friends might have known that I wasn't drinking, but they had no way of knowing how nervous I was. How hypervigilant I was. How much I worried about them, about the consequences of one shot too many, one late night too late. Sobriety felt like a prison that I chose to be in, a way to feel some sense of control. I let myself feel my anxiety and told myself that I should be able to deal with it, even there, without the help of alcohol. That I should be able to handle my issues on my own. That I should be able to make friends and fit in without giving in.

The novelty of college parties wore off fast. Those with a clear mind could see how primitive they were. Nobody talked or socialized—the music was loud enough to keep everyone from thinking. From the corner of dorm rooms, I watched my friends, playing along as they passed around placenta-looking bags filled with Franzia, aka the cheapest wine they could get their hands on. When my friends gagged at the taste of Bankers Club Vodka, it made me wonder if they truly hated themselves. Unsurprisingly, the situation would often escalate. With a pit in my stomach, I watched my friends—ones I won't name because their mothers would kill them—head off into bathrooms. There, they snorted lines of coke handed off to them by heirs and nepo babies—people I wished they would steer clear of. I watched them glance over at me quickly before turning away and toward the people they got high with. They were too drunk to see a random pair of scissors sticking out of a couch, waiting to impale them as they swayed. I snatched up the scissors and threw them away. *I don't want to be the caretaker or the responsible one,* I thought. *I don't want them to avoid me in the same way that they avoided their parents after their first beer, their first time sneaking out, the first time they did something they'd been told not to do. They won't remember the scissors in the couch or the times that I picked them up from a party where they could barely walk. They'll remember not to invite me the next time.*

Eventually somebody threw a cup in the air and beer inevitably flew through the crowd, spraying my hair. I stood to the side of the room and checked my email because I didn't know what else to do. Every party was the same. When I got overwhelmed, I'd say goodbye to a couple of people who wouldn't remember that I had even been there. Next to the door, I'd step over yet another pile of black Canada Goose coats, thrown carelessly in the corner, discarded by drunk partygoers who would likely forget they brought them.

I remember the first time I looked up the price of the Canada Goose jackets that seemed to litter the campus. At first I thought they might be a cheap, popular jacket—something *everyone* and their mom had. But when Richard and I decided to look up the price of these jackets, we were both dumbfounded. *That basic-ass black jacket with a little red patch? ONE GRAND?*

And yet there they were, always piled up and stepped on. I resisted the urge to take one, knowing that nobody would notice or care or think anything of my grabbing a coat on my way out. I imagined that such a coat would keep me warmer than the one I'd brought from Arizona. I toyed with the idea of stealing it, keeping it, or selling it on eBay. Instead, I passed by them, moving through a campus riddled with parties exactly like the one I just left.

By the end of the school year, I stopped getting invited out as much, and when I did, I rarely went. When I would go, the anxiety I felt was debilitating, making me paranoid and jittery. Like clockwork, my chest would tighten and I'd struggle to breathe, feeling the crowded room closing in on me. I'd have to leave, no longer out of boredom but out of the need to survive. The community who used to give me life was sucking me dry, and I questioned if not drinking was worth all of this. I was afraid of being out of control if I drank, but at the same time I felt like I had no control over the anxiety that crippled me.

I didn't understand what was changing and why. I had been the extroverted, fun girl who wanted to do everything and meet everyone, and now I was becoming the quiet, withdrawn girl who left parties early, too anxious to be around others and too anxious to be alone. I wanted to lighten up, but my mind wouldn't let me. So I distracted myself from feeling left out and overwhelmed by searching for boarding schools for Fer, making lists of what he'd need to apply.

Maybe that was the difference. After college, I'd have a teenager with me in some capacity, one whose parents would be in another country, unable to enter this one; a teenager who I was solely responsible for. Maybe that's why I couldn't let loose. The stakes were higher.

I was taking a course called Democratic Insecurities, a writing seminar that everybody is supposed to get an A in, and in one of the last classes of the semester I raised my hand to ask a question. "Can you explain hegemony?"

Before I could focus on the professor's answer, Jeff, a kid who was always drunk out of his mind at the frat parties, muttered, "How do you *not* know what that is?" in an arrogant tone only a rich white boy can use. In any other time in my life, I would've channeled my mom's feistiness and fired back at him with a comment that empowered me and put him in his place, letting him know that I couldn't be fucked with like that. But my academic life was falling apart as much as my social life, so instead I sat still, shocked, second-guessing myself, my capabilities, and my intelligence.

I hadn't cared much about the first test I failed. I was in college, after all, so there would be so many more chances and this one test wouldn't break my grade. Plus, I needed straight As to get here, but I didn't need them once I was here. I figured that I could simply study harder. I figured I had failed my bio test because I had stepped on the giant compass in the middle of Locust Walk, triggering the bad luck "curse" of Penn folklore. But then the curse continued to affect me. I failed another test and butchered another assignment. I was struggling in classes that should have been easy, but none of my old techniques worked. I drank Red Bull and studied deep into the night. I went to office hours. I asked for help. My econ professor told me that there was nothing she could do for me. My lab instructor told me to pay more attention to the readings. I wondered if I was inherently dumb. Had I tricked Penn into accepting me? Was I really only a checkmark for affirmative action? In high school, I'd had so much more to think about—food, money, transportation, shitty sleep patterns, all on top of school. And here I had a living space, food from the dining hall every day, and a full-ride scholarship. I was in a perfect position to worry less, but it was as if my mind was more comfortable in the turmoil of overthinking, and it could never stop churning.

For so long college was the end goal, but the goalposts kept moving and I still had to compete for seats in classes, for internships, for baseline scholarship grades, and for prerequisite courses in my major. And I was competing with people who could afford to get wasted every weekend, do lines of coke, and throw their nine-hundred-dollar jackets on the stained floors of frat houses.

The playing field was actually a battlefield. Battlefields are never level.

23

BETTY CROCKER'S RECIPE
FOR SUCCESS

You have to get your GPA up—that's your ticket to landing an internship.

   Maybe if you weren't such a lazy shit.

You have to get an internship—that's your ticket to securing a job.

   Except you're actually incompetent.

You have to get a job—that's your ticket to providing for your family.

   It will never be enough.

Your brother is a teenager and has lost most of the English he knew. You have to bring him back here so he can have the same opportunities you have.

   This is an uphill battle you won't win.

How dare you even think of your family as a burden?
You're a terrible daughter.

Your parents are getting older. How much time do you even have left with them? Why would you choose to be away from them for so many years when you don't know how much longer they even have?
Leaving them was selfish. You only have yourself to blame.

B esides all the researching, analyzing, studying, and memorizing that comes with getting a degree, I had a constant undercurrent of uninvited thoughts. Thoughts that didn't give me a heads-up that they were coming and didn't knock at the door when they arrived. Thoughts that barged in like a cousin you hadn't seen in years, expecting to be fed, entertained, and kept company. I didn't have time for these visits. In fact I began to not have time for any kind of visits—from my thoughts, from my friends, or phone calls from my family. I needed to focus even if focusing was proving to be the hardest thing for my mind to do.

I tuned out the noise the best at Huntsman Hall, one of the few buildings on campus that was open twenty-four hours a day, and a part of the prestigious and exclusive Wharton School of Business at Penn. Huntsman had a gorgeous interior and beautiful private study rooms. Globally, it is a place known as "one of the most sophisticated large-scale instructional centers of any educational institution in the world." But access to Huntsman was restricted to Penn's favorite children—the students who had been accepted into Wharton. Curious about what the hype was, I took some classes at Wharton, worming my way in through well-researched loopholes. Despite all of us being Penn students, Wharton had a way of making you feel like an outsider. Wharton students could reserve rooms in Huntsman and had access to free printing, recruiters, and listservs full of internship opportunities—opportunities the rest of us were never aware of even if we had the relevant experience and knowledge. Wharton professors could expense their pricey lunches with students, whereas the rest of us just went to lunch with our professors at the Penn hotel across the street, which was free for us once a month.

Though I was able to access Huntsman and take a few classes there, I couldn't reserve rooms or get free printing, unless I used my Wharton friends' log-in credentials to mooch off the resources. And of course I did, continuing to find ways to steal a little bit back. To help me focus, I'd lock myself in the Huntsman study rooms as often as I could, even when they smelled like stale McDonald's. There, I'd skip meals and chug energy drinks to complete assignments. Friends would join me at times, but somehow after several hours working side by side, they'd have completed essays and research papers and I would still be staring at a blank Word document. I couldn't make sense of it. *What the fuck am I doing?*

On-campus recruiting is coming up. Is your résumé updated?
You can do it later.

Do you even know how to do case interviews?
Are they really that hard?

Have you reached out to boarding schools to figure out what you need to do for Fer to apply?

You don't have enough time.

Do you think your dad will get cancer from the corrosive dust of the factory he worked in?

He doesn't have healthcare.

Why did you choose to come back to the United States without your family, leaving Fer behind to witness the explosive destruction of your parents' marriage?

Because you are a coward.

What kind of sister are you?

An undeserving one.

Are you ready for the econ midterm?

Face it, you'll never be good with numbers.

Four to six in the morning were the golden hours, the time when I got all my work done. Then the hunger subsided, not because I had eaten, but because my body had finally given up growling for my attention. Sleep deprivation gave way to another burst of energy. And of course, two hours before the paper was due, the pressure was most intense. It was by no means the recipe for health and wellness, but it was a familiar recipe. And exactly like before, it led to success.

My GPA went up, finally breaking the 3.0 barrier, which opened the doors to different resources—more scholarships from the Hispanic Scholarship Fund and admittance into clubs like Cipactli, the Latinx honor society. I was allowed into rooms I had been locked out of when my grades were too low, my potential reduced to my 2.9 GPA. But I could allow myself to feel that rage for only a few seconds, because this was not a system where you could fight the injustice of arbitrary cutoff points. Standing up to a professor or begging them for extra credit opportunities to boost your grade was as pointless as trying to convince a government official that you deserved to cross an arbitrary border.

So I followed my normal course, swallowing my feelings and keeping my GPA above their benchmark. I secured interviews for internships, ensuring I wouldn't be scrambling like I was my first summer at Penn, where I ended up interning with the Catholic Church of Philadelphia. I was withdrawn socially and emotionally, but I was engaged in the classroom and busy networking outside of it.

Over time the intrusive thoughts invaded my mind less often and left quicker when they did. My nights no longer consisted of sparring with my brain. The formula worked once again. I had successfully strangled enough of my mind that it had room only for vital human needs. And I had convinced myself that the only vital human need I had was achievement. I withdrew from friends, going weeks without talking to anyone, preferring to hole up in my room with a bowl of cereal as my only meal of the day.

Junior year, I finally felt like I had figured out a process that worked for me. Cindy and I, along with a few of our other friends, had decided to move off campus to a town house nearby in order to save money. I was excited about having my own room and staying organized in the new year, getting a fresh start. But my excitement lasted only three days before a stranger broke into our newly rented place. When the break-in happened, I was away, giving the burglar a chance to go through my things before escaping. Along with the laptop I used for school and the camera that I captured memories with, the intruder also took my sense of safety. For the first time in a long time, I felt unsafe in my own bed, which led to a stronger stream of dark thoughts that would plague me at night. Sometimes I would be triggered by a shadow or the sound of someone coming into the apartment. Other times, it happened unprompted. My fear registered in my body.

My chest tightened.
What is happening?

My breath became rapid and shallow.
You can't breathe.

I was suddenly covered in chills but starting to sweat.
What the fuck is happening?

My heart pounded on the bars of my ribs, trying to escape, eager to explode.
You're having a heart attack.

The walls of the room were closing in; my hands were tingling. I felt like I was going to throw up.
You are dying.

Oh my god, am I dying?

You're dying.

I had regular panic attacks, making it impossible for me to compartmentalize my emotions in the way that I was so used to doing. As they happened, I questioned whether I should call an ambulance. Eventually the attacks became so severe that they left me immobilized for days. After a few bad ones, I decided that I needed to do something. I finally got up the courage to go to Penn's on-campus Counseling and Psychological Services (CAPS). There they assigned me to an older white woman. "She'll be your counselor," the receptionist at the front desk had said, quickly handing me an iPad to fill out all of my information.

During my first assessment with her, I realized that she would never be able to understand what I was going through.

"What does it mean to be undocumented?" she asked naively. Wide-eyed, I went through the grueling task of educating her. By the time I left, I felt more frustration rather than relief. Weeks later, another panic attack came. This time, a feeling of dread made me wonder if it would be easier to end it all. I finally understood Maddie.

I lay awake the entire night, my eyes fixed on the drawer where I kept all my migraine medication. Shaken by my own thoughts, I went back to CAPS, hoping that I would be seen by someone else. Luckily, the counselor that saw me that day was pragmatic, explaining my experience to me in clinical medical terms. She listened empathetically while offering practical solutions that would help distract me while the attacks happened.

"Name five things you can see, four things you can touch,

three things you can hear, two things you can smell, and one thing you can taste," she said. "It will help ground you back in your surroundings." After taking a few notes, the counselor sent me next door to a psychiatrist. "I hope that you'll be open to what the doctor has to say," she continued. "Medications are really helpful for situations like yours."

Admittedly I questioned the ability of a pill to help control what I was feeling, but I was desperate, so I gave it a chance.

At first the changes were subtle and imperceptible. "That's normal," the psychiatrist said when I asked. "We want them to get you back somewhere neutral," she explained. "They're not going to make you happy from one day to the next." The psychiatrist was right. It wasn't always sunny in Philadelphia, but sometimes I was able to see a hint of light coming through the clouds. I felt lighter and was able to get myself up in the mornings. Sometimes I even had the motivation to make myself breakfast and go on a run next to the Schuylkill River, reminding me of my runs in Arizona along the river trails.

When I told my parents about the medication I was taking, they seemed surprised. "You're too young to be worried," my dad said. "Look at where you are." With time, I hoped that they'd be able to understand what it meant to have chemical imbalances in your brain. They had to because I knew they had them, too.

———————

After a few weeks of adjusting to my medication, I was back to pulling all-nighters in Huntsman in order to keep my GPA up. I also found myself looking for opportunities that would take me out of the Penn bubble. On the weekends, I traveled to different forums hosted across the Ivy League or attended a variety of different conferences, where I met former Mexican presidents and reporters like María Elena Salinas, Denise Maerker, and María Hinojosa—women whose accomplishments and drive pushed me to start writing.

I started with what I knew: my own story. As I put words to paper, I let myself feel proud of how far I'd come. Eagerly I sent off my story in an email to different publishers, hoping that someone might want to share it more widely. After the rush of sending it wore off, I crashed. When I woke up the next morning, my throat felt tight, as if I was swallowing knives. Unable to ignore the pain, I went to the doctor without even attempting to talk myself out of it.

The nurses didn't give a shit about my newfound passion for writing. They grilled me with the basics.

Do you smoke? Have you been on antibiotics recently? What about steroids? Do you have any medical conditions that affect your immune system, like AIDS or cancer? What about diabetes?

After the nurse made me gag with a tongue depressor and took some blood, we waited for the results. No strep.

How much alcohol do you drink? How many glasses of water per day are you drinking? What about sleep—how many hours do you get? Are you eating a well-balanced diet?

After confessing that I wasn't necessarily the poster child for wellness, that I was pulling all-nighters more often than not and fueling up on Red Bull and cereal, she stuck another tongue depressor in my mouth. The result proved her new hypothesis. My immune system was so weak that the normal bacteria that lives on our skin and in our body was taking over my mouth and throat, causing an infection.

"You have a yeast infection," the nurse told me. "In your throat." With a mirror, the nurse showed me the spores I'd cultured in the back of my throat. "We usually only see this in newborns," she continued. "Because they have such frail little immune systems." I would have been fascinated if I hadn't been completely nauseated.

"Babies don't have deadlines," I replied, making the nurse chuckle.

After a lecture on the importance of taking care of myself, eating a balanced diet, and getting enough sleep, I left the doctor's office with a prescription for a fourteen-day dose of an antifungal medication, along with some cough syrup with codeine to "encourage" me to sleep. If only she could've prescribed something for my stubbornness. Because even as I walked out of that office, I knew that the so-called healthy lifestyle I needed to adopt was not feasible in a place like Penn, where your future hinges on exclusive access—knowing the right people, saying the right words, projecting an image of success, and displaying the image of prestige.

I finished the antifungal medication but took only two doses of my codeine-laced cough syrup before I was back to my ways. Back to creating the kind of life-or-death pressure that—in spite of crippling anxiety, intrusive thoughts, and a weak-ass immune system—I had convinced myself I thrived under; the kind of stress and chaos that were my norm and were therefore essential ingredients in my recipe for success.

24

WHICH WORLD WILL I CHANGE?

Before I'd even committed to going to Penn, the on-campus photographers roaming around during admitted-student visitation days had snapped a picture of me. In hindsight I shouldn't have been surprised to now see my face plastered all over their website and social media pages. My Brown skin, my bright smile, and the green and yellow Brazilian scarf I'd bought during my trip with National Geographic made this photo the quintessential marketing tool for the majority white college. The fact that I was holding a sign that read *At Penn I Will Change the World* was icing on the optics cake. If anything, I was more surprised that they didn't use #diversity to seal the deal. Back then, I was still drunk on hope and ambition, naive to the cutthroat nature of prestige schools. As I scrolled the comments left below my picture, one stood out.

"I used to think I could change the world, too—that won't last long."

I rolled my eyes and allowed the comment to get under my skin—but only because under my skin was the storehouse for all the other snide remarks and offhand insults that begged me to prove them wrong.

"You should go back to Mexico with your family."

"You don't *need* to be valedictorian."

"There's no such thing as full rides."

"Girls like *you* don't go to places like *that*."

Under my skin, the assembled doubts were like gasoline on the fire that fueled my achievement.

But the thing is, when I had first filled out that poster and smiled for that picture, I actually believed that at Penn, I would change the world. The fact that I had gotten into a school like Penn gave me confidence that I was going to do something big, something that made a difference. I looked at impact in tiers. You can be an EMT, the first on the scene of a car accident or medical emergency. You're helping people, but not to the extent that the next tier does. The next tier has the doctors and nurses who help thousands of people in their career. Then there are further tiers, on which there are scientists who help make drugs or lifesaving vaccines for ideally the whole world. But then there are even more tiers—for example, the politicians who decide who has access to those vaccines and how they get distributed. You can be in law and politics and change the way healthcare works, ensuring that everybody gets a certain standard of care, which changes the entire trajectory of society. I wanted to do the most that an individual could do to help people. I wanted to be the poster child representing the successful daughter of immigrants. I wanted to be in the top tier of people who were changing the world.

That wide-eyed optimism didn't last long at Penn. Semester after semester, I was faced with the crushing reality of capitalism and nepotism, so that by the time recruitment for internships and postgraduate jobs rolled around, I was sobered by the impossible nature of systems perpetuating poverty. I also felt limited by what I could do, even at a personal level. My reality was one in which my little brother would eventually end up in my care. He'd come to the United States as soon as I graduated, and eventually I'd turn into not only his caregiver but also the caregiver for my aging parents. I faced bills and laws that I couldn't affect. The pressures of my everyday life rapidly sent me into a whirlwind of existential nihilism. Before college I didn't even know what *nihilism* meant.

At some point during junior year, I decided that I would study abroad. I had always wanted to do this, but the program required that I have a summer internship lined up before I committed to it. Although I was tired of the ways my potential was being measured by minute fluctuations in my still-not-that-high GPA, I played the game and began to qualify for help that I had needed from the beginning. I attended more conferences, and suddenly there was more access to mentorship. Through the Hispanic Scholarship Fund, I received business coaching and leadership training. Somehow HSF had managed to create a three-day crash course on how to become a professional—aka get a job after college. It didn't take long for me to discern the pattern of the game. Interviews, applications, and résumés were all handled in specific ways that could be replicated and repeated across industries. Ruth, a staff member at HSF, had told us to aim big.

"If you don't ask, you don't get," she said. "You have what it takes to get to where you need to go." Afterwards, staff would run us through typical questions asked by recruiters:

"Tell me about yourself."

"When was there a time when you overcame a challenge?"

"What are your two weaknesses?"

Little by little, I caught on to the formula, internalizing it in a way that made sense to me.

STEP 1. TELL THEM WHERE YOU'RE FROM, BUT ADD A LITTLE *CHILD OF IMMIGRANT SPICE*

"I was raised in Tucson, Arizona, by immigrant parents. They always taught me the value of education and hard work and . . ."

STEP 2. EMPHASIZE HOW THAT SPICE MADE YOU STRONGER FOR #IMPACT

"I got to put those lessons into practice when they went back to Mexico during my freshman year of high school. I persuaded my parents to let me stay in the States, confident in the doors that an American education would open. After I graduated as valedictorian of my class, my journey—which is my family's journey as well—led me to a school like Penn."

STEP 3. GAS THE COMPANY UP

"All these challenges made me the resilient person I am today. At a company like yours, I know that I will be able to succeed, given my drive and my ability to problem-solve. I'm so excited for a future in which I'm part of the team."

STEP 4. LOCK IN THE MONETIZATION OF TRAUMA

*"Yes, I would love to work with your team! While the offer
is generous, I think that my level of experience substantiates a
higher base pay. Would you be willing to go up twenty percent?"*

When a social media tech giant asked, "Why do you want to
work here? Why are you a good fit for this position?" I answered,
"Your company is connecting people. People like my family who
are separated by borders. When I lived in the United States without my parents, direct messages on your app were the way we
stayed in contact. So while I know that I bring the level of skill
and expertise to work with the team efficiently and effectively, I
also know that I want to be a part of the bigger picture that you
are painting. I want to be a part of the level of impact that your
company has had on keeping people connected despite all the
barriers and borders that try to disconnect them."

When I'd interview in the banking world, I'd answer their
questions the same way. "Tell us how our company aligns with
your passion and professional goals," the recruiters pried. Confidently I'd start my answer. "I have always been interested in
how money works and moves across the world," I would begin
before leading into the personal experiences I'd had that made
it so. "Growing up along the border, I always saw my parents
discussing the fluctuation between the Mexican peso and the
U.S. dollar." Then I'd tie it up with a little knot that highlighted
my pretentious Ivy League education. "When I got to Penn, I
made it my goal to understand the mechanics of international
economics. I'd love to continue learning and growing at your
company." Once I was done, I'd read the recruiter's face, search-

ing for clues in their expression in the same way that they looked for clues in my résumé.

Sometimes I would nearly fool *myself* with the stories and answers I'd come up with. *Maybe I do want to work here,* I would think. But I really didn't want to be at these places. At Penn, getting an internship at Goldman Sachs or Morgan Stanley served as a sort of social signal. Even students who could have spent their whole lives living in $5,000-a-month apartments paid for by their parents went after these jobs. For me, the reality was simple: I needed money, healthcare, and stability. I needed a place to bring my brother to once I brought him back into the United States.

Unsurprisingly, recruiters were interested in the version of myself that I gave them. The one that upheld the super-immigrant narrative and kissed America's ass as the land of freedom and opportunity as long as you worked hard enough. Deep down, I hated the way I was commodifying my traumas—making them palatable to people and companies who cared only about revenue. And yet I still did it because I was good at it. Because it gave me access to power and spaces with money. Because these decisions, these stupid little interviews, could give me the foundation to change *my* world. But keeping up this facade was exhausting. On-campus recruiting was exhausting. Nobody cared about mental health. Nobody cared about grades or learning or the fact that we were at one of the top universities in the world. Penn's, and specifically Wharton's, pre-professional atmosphere turned us into soulless robots. Despite this, I craved validation from recruiters as much as everyone else did. They loved to hear how their company could play a potential role in my "overcoming" my trauma. I could use my story to get ahead. Once again, I thought I had cracked the code and figured out the formula, so when it came time to get Fer into a boarding school in the United States, I felt confident that the same formula would work for him, too.

The moment that I left my brother behind in Mexico, I knew that I had to bring him back. There wasn't a day that I didn't think about him and about the decisions I'd made because of his absence. His loss had always seemed like the most devastating outcome of shitty policies against immigrants. In Mexico, he faced educational gaps, language barriers, and lack of access to the public resources I'd grown up using in America. I knew that if he stayed in Mexico, he would never be a competitive applicant for U.S. colleges. The only Mexicans at Penn that weren't immigrants but actually had gotten in *from* Mexico were rich and had gone to elite private schools in big cities. My brother was wasting away in the middle of the desert in the violent little narco town my parents had grown up in. If I didn't bring Fer back to the U.S.—back to me—I knew he'd be royally fucked. I couldn't imagine what his future would be, but having seen the sparkle in his eye, his visible intelligence, and his impeccable comportment, I had to do everything I could to give him a chance.

Still, the idea of being a twenty-something in charge of a teenager terrified me, so I looked at alternatives for my brother in the same way my parents had done for me when I was growing up. Between classes, I spent time researching the obnoxious boarding schools many of my classmates had gone to.

Choate (*who TF names a school like that and then pronounces it like that?*), Andover, Exeter . . . they were all expensive, but I figured every once in a while they'd have scholarship options or financial aid. So I did what I had done for myself. I emailed and packaged his trauma as best as I could. I explained how he was ripped away from his education, friends, sister, and country. I talked about how he was bilingual until he was eight years old but emphasized how quickly he would regain his English once he was back. I tried to tie up our parents' separation, that would sometimes turn violent, into a pretty little bow. Having Fer at a boarding school would allow his needs to be met by people who were experts in helping children learn and flourish. Selfishly, it also meant that I could have an independent post-college life. But again and again enrollment counselors rejected him, and I found myself on the cold floors of Huntsman having public meltdowns over shit nobody around me could even come close to comprehending.

How could I have everything and Fer have nothing? Before he even moved here, I felt like I was failing him. Why wasn't the formula that worked for me working for him? Why was my story moving and impactful, the perfect balance of sad and inspiring, and yet Fer's was confusing, harder to track, and didn't land with the same impact? I guessed there were tiers of impact when it came to trauma, too.

Eventually these rejections forced a decision on me—one that I had been trying to prepare for since the day I'd said goodbye to him for the first time at the border. After I graduated from college, Fer would come and live with me. I'd enroll him in public school, and instead of having his meals prepared in a commercial kitchen by a chef and eaten in a dining hall with his peers, he'd have meals cooked by his sister, who often ate cereal for dinner.

The process of telling our stories—whether in interviews or on boarding school applications—came at a cost. When I first told my story, in the Religious Action Center in D.C., and when I told it again in the essay I'd emailed off and eventually got published on NPR's *Latino USA,* I was still sensitive to it. I still had feelings of sadness, anger, and longing. But after a grueling semester focused on recruiting, I had told my story hundreds of times in interviews, on scholarship applications, and in speeches. I had helped tell Fer's story in countless phone calls and essays. My words no longer carried any emotional weight. Even the ways I paused and emphasized certain parts of my story were calculated to get the response I needed. My story mattered to other people, but it no longer mattered to me. I was desensitized to what we had been through, numb to the ways it affected us, and ignorant of the ways it was still affecting us.

But all that desensitization paid well. I accepted a job at Wells Fargo—before it was publicly considered a corrupt bank—securing my post-college income and a move to New York City. While many of my friends freaked out over finding a job, I slowed down and went abroad, exploring my little heart out in London. There I went out on dates with British and French boys who may or may not have fetishized me for being Mexican. Not all, but definitely some. The reality was that I didn't care. My next steps were planned for me, so I did what I wanted. I took classes that excited me, like Latin American art history, where, after years of being in school, I finally got to focus on my culture. I learned about how art was used by the Spanish to impose Christianity and how Indigenous artists left hidden messages within their art, covertly affirming their existence through symbolism. More important, I learned how people who rebelled through art and politics were behind each image. I saw anger, sadness, and happiness. I saw windows to the almost mythical past my heritage was tied to.

The beginning of my time at Penn was filled with idealism. I had the energy and motivation, and the naivete, to believe with all my heart in my ability—in my generation's ability—to change the world. But my four years at college flew by and were filled with heart-wrenching realizations. Each question opened up a new Pandora's box. The world's problems were too big for me or any one other individual to solve. Sitting beside some of my friends during graduation didn't inspire me in the way that I thought it would. We were separated by major and by school throughout most of the ceremonies, with Ivan and the rest of the Wharton students listening to different speakers than we did in the College of Arts and Sciences, which I was a part of after majoring in philosophy, politics, and economics. We were united only by our black caps and gowns and the corporate jobs we had lined up. While I waited for my turn to walk the stage, I wondered which of my beautiful friendships would survive into adulthood. I wondered which would stay deep and meaningful, and which would become nothing more than sterile professional connections.

The ceremony—the process of graduating—wasn't what I'd dreamed of as a kid. It was grueling and bitter. Our commencement speaker was Andrea Mitchell, an NBC reporter who had donated money to Penn. I didn't know who she was even after looking her up on Google. Her speech was full of clichés, and it wasn't long before I tuned her out. What could she possibly say to make me feel better? What could she possibly say to a crowd of newly sold-out students? Our hearts belonged to the Goldman Sachses and BCGs of the world. Under the hot sun, I alternately dozed off and reminisced about the small moments that had brought me happiness at Penn. The architecture and the trees along Locust Walk, the rooftop of Van Pelt Library, and the eerie lounges I'd hung out in in the Quad. I thought about my classes. I wished that I could have been more present and less pressured.

Surrounded by the smartest people I'd ever met, I wished that I'd had more time to revel in the magic of learning. I wish we all had. I wondered if everyone was asking themselves what the fuck they were doing. I wondered if anyone else had regrets. Were we depleted of the things that we once loved and truly headed toward a path of corporate doom? Were we saving the world or perpetuating the systems that already existed?

At Penn I Will Change the World.

"I used to think I could change the world, too—that won't last long."

As the weather transitioned from half sunny to half rainy, I scanned the crowd of spectators who were there to watch their loved ones graduate. I scanned each row until I found the faces that, despite time and distance, would always be familiar. Though she sat far away in the crowd, I could make out the thickness of my mom's eyebrows. She sat right next to my twiggy teenage brother. Although my dad wasn't able to be there, my mom had miraculously gotten her tourist visa renewed in time for my graduation. I looked back to the stage with resolve.

I wasn't going to change *the* world, but I was going to change *their* world.

25

WORKING SISTER

The week after I graduated from Penn, I showed my mom and Fer around Philadelphia, introducing them to the life I had lived and the city I had called home for the past four years. We went to the Liberty Bell, ran up the famous steps featured in *Rocky*, checked out the art museum, and of course went to a famous Mexican barbacoa restaurant in South Philly.

"They make it just like they do in the South of Mexico," my mom remarked as she bit into a taco, juice from the meat running down her hands. Before the reality of transitioning from college to my career set in, we simply enjoyed one another's company. Despite my uneasiness about starting a job that I wasn't excited for or about becoming my brother's legal guardian, I tried to remind myself that my degree was worth a quarter of a million dollars and that I could do it. I'd had a privileged education, one that could never be taken away. Eventually I sent Mom and Fer back on an airplane to Mexico for the summer. A few days later, I got on a flight to Charlotte, North Carolina, where the training for my new banking job would take place. During my time there, I spent my days thinking about stocks and bonds, my nights scrolling through StreetEasy looking for a place to live that was cheap and safe for both me and my brother. Although my mom would be able to visit us once Fer came to live with me permanently, the responsibility of raising him would fall on me—the oldest, the one who allegedly had her shit together.

At some point during my two months of training, I also began to wonder what I'd actually be doing while on the job. While my colleagues had drinks and chats with their managers, I never did. In fact, after emailing back and forth with my hiring manager, I wasn't even sure what team I'd be placed on. That, in addition to the complete clusterfuck that it was to find an affordable apartment in New York that (1) didn't look like shit and (2) looked *OKAY* enough online for me to sign a lease without visiting the place first, threw off my already wack brain chemistry, leading to anxiety and another bout of panic attacks. As the training sessions finished up, I signed a lease with Ramón, a classmate from Penn who was working in consulting and who hopefully would never be around. Ramón would have me and my brother as roommates. It wasn't ideal, but it would have to work.

On a sunny day in August, I packed my bags and boarded a flight to New York while my new job kept ghosting me about the details of my position. Exasperated, I tried to let it go and began the task of finding a school for my little brother, who had flown in with my mom to New York on the same day I did. Moving isn't easy to begin with, but add in a worried mother who speaks no English and has never been to New York City along with an anxious teenager about to enter a shitty public school system and you truly have a bad situation. Although I had mounds of personal business to attend to, I was quickly forced into work mode as my first day at the office loomed.

It wasn't until I finally walked through the office door that somebody finally spoke to me—Octavia, a saleswoman with a clean short blond bob and dressed in a modern suit, who had helped run the internship the summer before. After a few formalities, she led me to the right corner of the office, where a group of mostly women sat bolt upright while typing on their triple monitor setups.

"This is your new team," Octavia said, "and this is Larry, your supervisor. He works in Corporate Access." Half turning in his chair, Larry greeted me.

"Welcome, I'll go ahead and let the girls brief you on everything." With that, he turned back to his computer screen. Larry was a bald white man who wore the same light blue button-down and navy chinos that everyone else did. It was an outfit worn everywhere across Midtown, making it feel like an unplanned school uniform. The women, who up until that moment hadn't glanced up, finally reacted with flat smiles.

"How does coffee sound?" a woman who I later learned was named Meredith chirped. "We'll give you the rundown."

On the way to the nearby café, it became clear that Meredith was the cheerleader of the group. She was a mom with a toddler—very #girlboss. Then there was Rachel, who was short and to the point, and Nina, who gave me frazzled-duck vibes (I think it was her hair?). For the next thirty minutes I tried to understand what the hell the Corporate Access department did and what they expected from me. None of them seemed prepared for my arrival and yet all of them had a firm opinion about how I should handle the job—which I eventually determined was a glorified role to handle logistics for rich people. The honeymoon phase lasted a total of one week before Rachel went on a two-week PTO and gave me all her projects, warning me to handle them to perfection before I'd even had a chance to talk to Larry about expectations and on-the-job training.

Meredith and Nina—who both acted as if they were my direct managers—kept close tabs on me. I watched their already nonexistent lips purse when I took calls arranging for my brother's school enrollment, and I got the silent treatment when I took PTO for court hearings in order to become his legal guardian. They asked for explanations they weren't entitled to by casting themselves as my mentors, as if they were trying to instruct me in the difference between right and wrong. Little by little, I felt them turn up the heat—as if I was a frog slowly getting boiled to death. I already felt isolated as the only Latina on the floor, but the girls took it a step further by discouraging me from speaking to the other teams or to new hires. Then came the incremental criticism of my work.

- *When I speak to you, it feels like I'm speaking to a wall.*
- *If I had made a mistake like the one you did, I would have left the office crying.*
- *Watch yourself.*
- *Oh, you feel sick? Tell Larry—I'm not your manager.*
- *Get off your phone.*
- *You need to be in the office earlier.*

- *Don't listen to music.*
- *Stop going out for lunch.*
- *Oh, wow, is that a new bag?*

I tried to leave work at work, but my phone pinged constantly with reminders and demands. Eventually I learned to keep my laptop around and be ready for whatever needed to be sent out, be it at 4 A.M. or 10 P.M. On top of it all, I tried to be there for Fer as he adjusted to a local public school in Brooklyn only a few minutes away from our new apartment.

Fer and I began our days around the same time, with me trying to wake up a little bit earlier to beat him to the bathroom we shared. (Ramón had his own bathroom, thank god.). Despite the fact that I was always yelled at for being late at work, my brother always beat me, delaying my start while I panicked and shouted at him.

"Apúrate, Fer! I'm going to be late," I would scream from outside the door.

"Why are you always trying to come in here as soon as I need the bathroom?" he said.

The mornings were a whirlwind. While I tried to find a work outfit that would make my coworkers jealous, Fer ironed his shirts, making sure he'd leave the house looking immaculate. We rarely had time to sit together and eat cereal, but we always tried walking out to the Q train together—him in tennis shoes and me in corporate heels. As soon as we were on the train, we put our headphones on, nudging each other whenever we saw people doing weird shit.

"Did you see the book that person is reading?" I whispered,

looking toward an old man reading a book titled *Do Androids Dream of Electric Sheep?*

"No, I'm too busy trying to avoid the weird puddle over here," he replied. Together, we would try to shut out the noise of the city, standing side by side on the moving train before we jumped off on different stops.

At school, Fer spent his mornings playing catch-up, fumbling through classes because his school didn't provide him with English as a Second Language services. In the office, I found closets and empty offices where I could quickly take phone calls to curse out his school.

What do you mean, you put Fer in AP Spanish? He's Mexican, *why would he need that?*

I couldn't give two shits that you don't want to give him ESL—it's an entitlement to all students who need it.

After my calls, I walked past the traders and the salespeople— the ones in the roles I thought I'd have—and back to the Corporate Access den of snakes. I spent my mornings working with C-suite executives and investors, setting them up for adult playdates where they would sit together in glass rooms surrounded by catered food to do business. In other words, I spent my mornings sucking up, kissing ass, and being as hospitable as possible to people with a level of wealth I would never access.

At lunch, I'd either steal catering or get a two-dollar can of tomato soup from CVS that I could heat up in the break room. Every once in a while I'd splurge on a Mexican food truck that made egg tacos, even offering to get some for the team in hopes that one of them would pay the whole bill. Other times, I'd walk alone to a cafeteria across the street frequented by the suited men of Park Avenue. While they ignored the cooks and briskly asked for meals, I was greeted with "Mi amor" and "Cómo estás, mija?" from the Mexicans flipping omelets.

My conversations with those guys kept me going. They reminded me of home, of my family, of my dad. They worked so hard, spent so many hours on their feet, serving food infused with love and culture to people in the Financial District who didn't treat them like people. They complimented my "fancy" outfits and asked me about work.

"Sigue adelante," they'd say. "Puro éxito!" Their excitement and warmth kept me going and reminded me again of my privilege. My coworkers saw them as the low-life boys I always "flirted" with. I saw them as my family. They were my dad, my cousins, even my brothers.

While I worked, my mom and brother became an inseparable duo. Because Mom was unable to understand the subway system, Fer showed her around. When I worked late nights at the office, she cooked, making sure that he was well fed. Coming back to an apartment that smelled like Mexican food with my mom and brother at the table was priceless. Still, I was uneasy about having my mom around, conscious of the fact that Ramón was our roommate and that he hadn't signed up to live with so many people. Not that Ramón minded that much—he was always on work trips, and when he was around, my mom would feed him. Still, when my mom's return flight to Mexico came around, Fer had a meltdown. Though I could have figured out a way to move her flight, I didn't. I knew full well that she'd need to go back eventually because of her visa. It was better for it to happen sooner rather than later.

When Mom left, Fer inevitably became more dependent on me. It didn't take long for him to have my work phone on speed dial. Every day, he would call, interrupting my work, and on the call he'd let me know what he was going to be doing after school or ask if he could use some of the money I gave him for food to buy his friend something from Dunkin' Donuts.

"Fer, I told you, don't ever ask me if you can buy food for someone. You know the answer. It's always yes. I would rather us go into debt than have you or anyone you know skimp on food and be hungry."

The food insecurity that I experienced in high school was still affecting me years later. In seasons of stress, I'd forget to eat, and when I'd remember, I'd remind myself how long I had made it without sustenance, convincing myself that I could make it a little while longer until I finished whatever task I was doing. Despite treating myself that way, I never wanted Fer to experience the hunger that I did. I never wanted his friends to experience it, either.

Because Fer would be home from school for a couple of hours before I got home from work, I'd turn down invitations to happy hour, choosing instead to spend the train ride decompressing from the toll that work—and the facade I had to maintain—took on me. Every day I put on my noise-canceling headphones and tried to forget the microaggressions I'd received that day.

- *Chica Elizabeth, let's go!*
- *You're not one of the AOC supporters, are you?*

- *You know, the thing about diversity is that those hires never end up being that good.*
- *Oh! You're Mexican? I had a Puerto Rican girlfriend.*

On the train, I let the anger and sadness I felt at work come to the surface, getting it out before making it home and sprawling on the couch. I envied the other young single professionals who had the energy to go out after work and the ones who got to come home to empty apartments or apartments with roommates that they weren't responsible for. I envied the ones who weren't working sisters, coming home to ensure their teenage brother's homework was done and that his stomach was full.

At the same time, life had taught me that conflicting feelings can coexist, because as much as I envied the people who weren't in my shoes, I treasured being able to be a part of Fer's life. Sure, I'd grumble through making him food, annoyed that he couldn't do it himself. But then Fer would do something stupid and make me laugh or offer to help me do laundry and clean and make me cry. Fer kept me together, helping me push dark thoughts away by reminding me of the things I loved. Together we watched *Fleabag* after dinner, screaming over the Hot Priest and the breaking of the fourth wall. In the craziness that was our life in the city, we found things that brought us comfort.

When I passed out from exhaustion, Fer would continue forward on his own, answering calls from my mom or finishing his homework. Sometimes I'd pretend to be fully asleep so my mom wouldn't ask for me. Instead, I'd listen to Fer updating my parents on the day-to-day.

"She's asleep . . . she seems happier lately."

"I'll ask her tomorrow if she can send the rent money."

"I'll take care of her. I love you, too."

At five-thirty the next morning, we'd start all over again. The repetitive nature of the week drained us, but Fer and I found ways to make the most of it. We watched *Jimmy Kimmel Live!* and shopped the thrift stores on the weekends. We pissed each other off, yelling at each other to take out the trash. Our parents were thousands of miles away, but we had each other, and we had New York's energy to keep us going.

———————

Despite the fact that we moved our office into the newly opened, pristine 30 Hudson Yards—the skyscraper that our corporation invested in and loaned more than a billion dollars for—the tantrum-throwing salespeople and the polyester-bloused snake women were draining the living shit out of me. Every day felt like I was dipping my head in concrete, my neurons hardening through countless mindless tasks. I often found myself staring toward the floor-to-ceiling windows, where I could barely see the top of the Vessel—a 150-foot-tall structure of connected staircases intended to be a work of art and architecture. When it opened, tourists filled up the steps and snapped selfies with the city and the Hudson River as their background, but it didn't take long for it to be shut down. Within a year of the Vessel opening, three people had died by suicide, leaping to their death. Despite protests from citizens, city officials, and bereaved family members, those who constructed the Vessel failed to install the higher barriers that had been proven in other places—like the atrium of NYU's Bobst Library and the George Washington Bridge—to reduce suicide attempts.

The Vessel reminded me of my life's fragility and the ways our minds can play tricks on us. At times the contrast felt unbearable, to be in a state-of-the-art skyscraper filled with offices, a Neiman Marcus, and other designer stores, but with happiness and comfort still so far out of reach. Wealth and power couldn't save us from death. The longer I stared out at the Vessel, the more my mind lingered on its proximity and how easy it would be for me to walk up there.

If I stay here much longer, I will be the next one to jump.

After a year of living with Ramón, Fer and I moved to a two-bedroom apartment closer to Prospect Park. We needed the space and a private place where Fer and I could hash out all that needed to get done in order for him to be prepared for college. Though I tried my best, I found myself sighing in annoyance at his need for my help, snapping at him when he'd have a lazy day and being harsh when he'd open up about missing Mexico.

"Fer, we are not here for you to fuck around and do dumb shit with your friends," I'd nag. "I get that you're sad because you miss your friends in Mexico, but that's not why we're here." Frustrated with my lack of patience, my brother would start to tear up. Angrily he'd blink the tears back in before slamming the door to his room. Afterwards, I'd regret the things I'd said to him, remembering how my parents had yelled and had outbursts themselves, particularly my dad. I recognized my reactions to stress because I'd seen my dad have similar ones. After years of avoiding his calls, I finally reached out to him again. Even when I'd pushed my dad away, angry by the way he had handled his separation from my mom, he had kept supporting me, sending me endless messages through Facebook.

- *I love you, mija.*
- *Checking in to make sure that you're okay.*
- *I know you needed a pair of jeans; I found a coupon for you.*
- *I'm so proud of you.*
- *I just woke up, wanted to wish you a good day.*

More often than not, I'd left them unread, failing to respond as I rushed from fire to fire.

"Fer is mad at me again," I'd tell my dad over the phone in times of crisis. "I want him to do well." He listened, understanding the inevitable tension that came when time and money were lacking.

"I'll talk to him," he'd reply. "I know you're trying your best. One day he'll understand." Eventually Fer would unlock his door and come out of his windowless cave.

"I'm sorry I yelled at you," I'd tell him. "Let me see the essay you're working on."

Exhausted from another long day of work, I spent my evenings on the couch with Fer going over homework, the TV playing in the background as it had back when we lived in el cuartito.

26

EMPTY NEST

After a shit year, the air around the new decade felt like an opportunity for everyone to start over. Over dinners with friends, we talked about what we'd do differently. We were tired of our jobs, burnt out by bad managers and toxic coworkers. We looked for ways out, ways to pivot. For me, 2020 represented a milestone that I'd dreamt about for years. It was Fer's senior year, and that meant he could start the college application process. Even at work things felt like they were improving. I'd found mentors and supporters like Adam—an ex-Goldman badass—who, as a Black man, had worked three times as hard as the mediocre white men in the office.

Adam encouraged me to find sure proof and public ways to make my presence known. "The team you're on will never let you succeed," he said. "It's up to you to protect yourself and make your own name." Adam was a breath of fresh air—acknowledging the racism rampant in the industry and telling me how he'd had to get past the bullshit himself as a Black immigrant. During our coffee chats, he pointed out nepotism babies and provided context for why things ran the way they did.

"The more you climb up, the lonelier it gets," he said. Our conversations weren't easy, but they were always honest.

Eventually I started doing things that I knew would piss my Tory-Burch-ballet-flat-wearing coworkers off. Little by little, they began to see my face and name show up on the company's internal home page, and after different analysts and managers congratulated me, they'd reluctantly do the same. I found myself applying to give a TED Talk that would be sponsored and hosted in part by Wells Fargo. Knowing that my team wouldn't approve of it, I used my coffee chats with Adam to brainstorm themes and ideas that would help me get selected as one of thirteen speakers. I wanted to say something that mattered. I wanted to be honest and focus on the things that I cared about. I wanted to be selected as a speaker because I had something to say.

Why was I working at a job I hated? *For money to help support my family. For representation in a system that didn't want to see my family for who we were: humans.*

Why was I supporting my family? *Because my brother deserved the same opportunities I had, and my parents had sacrificed a lot to ensure that we had a different future than they did.*

A couple of months later, I was flown into Charlotte and fitted with a microphone on one side of a stage with giant red T-E-D letters as the backdrop. The whole ordeal was obnoxious and exhilarating. Before I went up to speak, I smirked as I thought about how much this would piss people off in the office. Once on the stage, I did what I'd done multiple times before. I looked for my mom, whom I had flown in for the event, and I introduced myself with my full name before really getting into it. Somehow I was able to cast shade on the recruiting process and the banking world while making everyone laugh before talking about the fucked-up ways society projects narratives onto immigrants.

At the end, people stood up to applaud as I walked offstage. My mom beamed and I reveled in the attention as countless people came up to introduce themselves and thank me for my speech. Eventually TED posted the talk on their home page, and it went viral. I went back to New York energized, hopeful that I'd had an impact, that my talk would inspire or help someone who had walked down similar paths. At work, I was congratulated by the entire floor while my team ignored the fact that I had been plastered on websites and had been recognized by top management. For a while, I thought that the high-profile nature of my TED Talk would keep me safe, but it didn't. A mere few weeks later, Larry sat me down for what I thought would be an opportunity to go over next year's goals. Instead, I was told that they wouldn't be renewing my work contract. In less than three months I'd need a new job. Larry went through somersaults justifying a decision that I figured was made so that he could hire a longtime friend onto the team. Through clenched teeth and tears, I sat in shock as I was told by my absent and spineless manager that he never thought I presented a "sense of urgency" for a job that my entire family relied on.

———————

I was on PTO when Larry called me only a week after our conversation.

"Hey, letting you know that this COVID thing is getting

serious," he said. "Keep working from home—no need to come to the office until things clear up." Things escalated quickly after that. There I was stuck during lockdown in a New York apartment with my mom, who had come back to the city with me after my TED Talk, my brother, and a new puppy. Things got tense, especially when our mailman passed away from the virus.

"Mama, no salgas. Robert, our mailman, was here in March, and he's gone in April," I said. "I refuse to let that happen to you or Fer."

For the first time in my career, I was able to multitask without getting reprimanded for it, keeping hundreds of tabs open as I searched for job listings. Briefly I contemplated checking out sugardaddy.com, but ultimately decided to reach out to recruiters instead. Despite the presence of death in the air, a sense of life flourished as well. It's always both. I didn't have to rush into the city, put on my professional facade, and spend my energy on meaningless office chatter. I was with two out of my three family members—my dad was still forbidden from entering the country, his absence a constant reminder of our reality. And despite having to wear a mask every time I went outside and changing out of my clothes as soon as I got home from the grocery store, I could breathe in a way I couldn't before.

I spent my days applying to the dwindling numbers of opening positions as hiring managers pared back their job postings the longer the lockdown went on. I spoke with recruiters, did mock interviews, and tried to remain hopeful, knowing that the worst-case scenario would be that we put all our stuff into a storage unit and head back to Mexico, in which case all this hard work for Fer would be for nothing. *No big deal, right?* I thought to myself. *It's fine. We're fine. Everything is fine.*

At night, my mom would make enchiladas or chipotle chicken over rice. Then we'd all pile onto the couch—our COVID puppy Yoshi snuggled right between us—and binge *Breaking Bad, Schitt's Creek,* and *Veep* with Spanish subtitles for my mom. And right before seven o'clock rolled around, we'd gather the pots and pans, open the windows, and bang them together as we whooped and hollered in gratitude for the healthcare workers on the front lines. In the greater community of New York and in the community of our family, we found ways to bring each other up. We weren't alone.

———

I don't know what changed for my corporation, but two weeks before my contract was set to expire, people from other teams and departments started reaching out to me. The head of the trading floor, Mitch, called me to ask how I was and let me know that he had some leads for me. Adam, who'd always had my back, let me know that prime brokerage had some openings. And Ted, one of the managers of the research analyst team, reached out to talk about the possibility of my working under an analyst. Was it because of the Great Resignation, when people were leaving their jobs in droves? Was it because the country was having a moment of racial reckoning when George Floyd was murdered, and corporations were rushing to cover their white asses by reassessing the (lack of) diversity of their team? Was it because I was a valuable employee who indeed did not lack urgency? I don't know what the reason was, but with recruiting and hiring coming to a near halt, I stayed on in the financial world, joining a new team in prime brokerage. Fer and I could stay in the city and finish what we set out to do.

The rest of Fer's senior year ended up being virtual. My mom stayed with us the entire time, unable to leave because of COVID. After a slightly tumultuous college application process that included too many rejection letters and a crushing weight of fear that I had let Fer down, he was eventually accepted into Middlebury College, one of his top choices despite its being in the middle of nowhere in Vermont. Ironically, I was away on a self-care trip with friends when the notification of his acceptance came— leaving Fer freaked out and alone when he first found out.

"I can't . . . I can't believe it," my brother gushed over the phone. "We made it."

Wheeling my bright orange and red suitcases across Penn's campus was fresh in my memory as I turned into one of those crazy middle-aged coupon ladies, clipping any and every relevant discount code for all the essentials Fer would need, and even for the things he might want. We got him nice bedclothes and all his bathroom essentials—he wouldn't have to walk across town to a Walmart—and I even convinced our super to sell us the mini fridge he kept in the basement. I had so much fun looking for sales, perusing the clearance section and presenting my coupons at the checkout.

When it came time to make the five-hour trek from New York to Middlebury, my friend Estefanía flew out to visit me and tagged along—mostly because we had plans after we dropped him off, but also because despite being wildly independent, I did not have my driver's license and we needed someone to drive the rental car. Estefanía came to our rescue, and we loaded up the car with Fer's things, our luggage, and my now two dogs, and we hit the road.

Middlebury's campus was beautiful, the neutral colors of the buildings bright against the backdrop of Vermont's changing leaves. I am not sure there is any place like Vermont in the fall. The Adirondack Mountains were visible to the west and the Green Mountains to the east, providing a visceral sense of protection. Middlebury's rural and scenic setting couldn't have been more different from Penn's but they both evoked a scholarly energy. The Reading Room in Middlebury's library resembled the old-world architecture of Penn and served as a reminder of the sturdiness of this place. I needed this place to be sturdy for my brother.

We took our time setting up Fer's room, even driving thirty minutes into Burlington to get some last-minute bins and snacks. Joking that we were Fer's moms dropping him off at college, we laughed together while making his bed, unpacking his clothes, and stocking his fridge. For our last meal together, we went to a delicious Thai place nearby and talked as if it were a normal Thursday night, as if it weren't the last meal we'd be sharing together for months. With full stomachs, after a full day, we drove him back to campus to say goodbye. And Fer calmly got out of the car and waved us off. It was the kind of goodbye we gave each other when he was getting off the Q train at his stop and I was staying on. The kind of goodbye we'd say when I'd leave his school, after a meeting with a teacher, and head back to work; the kind we said to each other after my graduation, knowing we'd be living together in only a few weeks. The kind I said to him every morning in Arizona when we went our separate ways to school.

It was the kind of goodbye we never got to say when my uncle picked him up that day and drove him to the border while I was sitting in class.

Fer has always been more sensitive than me, so in some ways it surprised me to have such an emotionless farewell. But in some ways, it might have been intentional, a distraction from the weight of the moment. I felt sadness knotting up my throat and tears filling my eyes, but I refused to let them fall.

"It's okay to cry," Estefanía gently reminded me from the driver's seat. I kept my eyes open, refusing even to blink, knowing that if I did the tears might spill over.

"No, no, I'm not going to cry."

Instead, I reminded myself that I was looking forward to my own space, to coming home after work and not having to make dinner for the bottomless pit that is a teenage boy's stomach. I reminded myself that it was finally *my* time to have some freedom, be a little more careless, and have a little bit more fun. I reminded myself that this was my time to enjoy everything I had worked for. I told myself to be happy and swallowed the knot of sadness.

27

UNBRIDLED CURRENTS

Camarón que se duerme, se lo lleva la corriente.
(The shrimp that sleeps is taken by the current.)
—Mexican Proverb

'd decided to leave finance and join the tech world as a product manager a few months before I had to drop Fer off at college. I didn't write a goodbye email or give any of my contact details. I simply *left*. My new role gave me something that I hadn't had since I'd started my job in banking: flexibility. With my brother well on his way to paving his own path, I thought about the different things that I could do. There were trips and places that I wanted to see. There were late-night comedy shows that I wanted to experience. Without the responsibility of another human, I had time to live. And still, I found myself going back to the one thing I craved the most—silence.

In the mornings, I woke up to an empty apartment except for my two eager puppies. With licks and cuddles, they nudged me out of bed for their morning walk. Once we were back, I filled their bowls and took a slow shower—no one else needed to shower after me. Even chores became somewhat enjoyable. My laundry didn't include heaps of my brother's gym clothes. The sink had only a few of my dishes. During the day, I took breaks in my work. I loved making sure that I was in the right spot, at just the right time, to bask in the midafternoon sunlight that spilled through my window and left a golden hue throughout the room. I loved the coziness of my couch, my place, my mind. These basic things—having my own schedule and routine, having quiet and solitude—had become luxuries, and I reveled in them.

I was present.

I was peaceful.

I was happy.

Though I still provided for my family by making my parents authorized users on my credit card and helped Fer with things that his financial aid package didn't cover, I let myself become my own person. I knew that as the eldest daughter in a Mexican family, I would always be tied to making sure that everyone else was well taken care of. Rather than dwelling on what that would mean for my future, I accepted the fact that I would become my parents' retirement plan. The knowledge that we were getting closer to the stability I had so desperately wished for growing up was enough to make me believe that it was worth it.

While enjoying the space I had created for myself, I set up safety nets that would help protect it. Rather than having my mom or dad work a minimum wage job for $3 an hour in Mexico, I sent them money, taking into account the value of their health and well-being. The risk of an injury or simply the long-term effects of hard labor on their bodies weren't worth it. Similar calculations were done to ensure my brother's well-being. Because he was still my legal dependent, I kept him enrolled on my healthcare plan despite having to pay more for his inclusion.

"Más vale prevenir que lamentar," my dad said. "Prevention is better than regret." By reading the fine print and filling out the paperwork, I was able to empty parts of my brain that had run nonstop thinking about everyone else's well-being. "Out of sight, out of mind," I told myself from the comfort of my couch I'd bought off Craigslist. I enjoyed the silence of my home, knowing full well that it would be interrupted by my brother's frequent calls from school.

When November rolled around, I knew that I needed to get to someplace warm. If I stayed in New York through the winter, I was sure that I'd never leave the apartment. My Mexican blood and Arizonan roots weren't built to withstand the bitter cold. While I had hoped that my first travel destination away from my refreshingly empty nest would be somewhere new, the never-ending pandemic meant that a lot of travel was still restricted. Pragmatically, I decided to head to Mexico, where I could visit my parents and grandparents after quarantining. The news of my return was exciting to everyone, especially my dad, whom I hadn't seen in years. I planned to stay with my family in Sonora for the coldest months over the holidays. If things became safer, the option of traveling internally within Mexico was a possibility as well. With luck, I'd come back to New York the next spring refreshed after having spent days basking along Mexico's coasts. With my dogs and a suitcase, I headed to JFK, well aware that no matter what I did, I'd always have excess baggage.

———————

Reunions with my family always feel like a special occasion, but then again, Mexican families can make *anything* feel like a special occasion. With boisterous greetings and emphatic storytelling, we go from bear hugs to giving one another a hard time in minutes. When we are together, there is an ease and there is always food. Not long after I arrived, extended family and neighbors started appearing for dinner.

Mexican meals aren't always beautiful. The plates aren't perfectly placed, and the colors don't complement one another. Sometimes Mexican meals have Styrofoam containers at the center of the table, but they are full of steaming tamales and bottles of watery hot sauce from the store. They sit there untouched until someone asks if there is something else. Then your great-aunt pulls out an old container of tomato paste that she cleaned up real good. A jar that she recycled and then filled with leftover salsa from the tacos she had two days ago.

Uncles and cousins move in and out of the tiny kitchen, hovering near the stove that once belonged to my great-grandmother. It's rusty in all the right places and sits beside a small window framed by ruffled, tacky but cute curtains. The curtains collect the smells of the kitchen, being covered in a thin layer of grease like everything else as food is cooked and leftovers are heated. I think about asking my aunt to make me a dress in the same print as the curtains.

I watch as everyone grabs the tamales and lays them out on their Styrofoam plates. They are a great meal for when you're on the go but a perfect meal when you have time to stay and enjoy the company. These tamales are Sonoran. They aren't filled with only meat or corn. They're filled with leftover beans and raisins and meat from the other day. It's a weird mix that shouldn't work, but it always does. My mom and I never learned how to make tamales, but while we have people that make them for us, we'll eat.

My plate is streaked with what's left of my refried beans, which form a paste that is not brown but nearly orange from the chiles my aunt mashed in. My great-aunt sits on the other side of the table, asking if I want more coffee. More beans. More. She tells me I can have her stove one day as my inheritance. She says nobody has claimed it yet. My mom grabs the tin container that's filled with sugar, and I mix a scoop into a diluted cup of coffee with the powdered creamer she gets from the United States. As we sit together, I notice that none of our cups match, but they warm our hands all the same.

A Mexican meal doesn't have to be beautiful to taste like home. And I am struck by how at home I feel, how normal I feel here. From the high of giving a viral TED Talk to the low of nearly getting laid off, I realize my life has been marked by extremes. As I sip my coffee, I remember something that my friend Ivan had told me in college after some sort of disappointment.

"I think the world is always balancing itself," he said. "When something really good happens, something difficult usually follows." Accepting this philosophy made it easier to digest reality, even if it meant that I would always be recovering from failure while pursuing success. As my mom told those at the table stories about my childhood, I thought about what she'd told me so long ago. *Remember, Elizabeth, you have to be the best.* Through sacrifice, I had made sure that I was. I stood out, beat systems, and cracked codes. I was an exceptional daughter, an exceptional example of immigrant success. But as I looked around the kitchen table that evening with my family, everything was so . . . *ordinary*. In Mexico, I was ordinary. I was another Brown girl, spending time with her family and making plans with her friends. This very sense of ordinariness indicated that I had officially run past the finish line, that I had left the constant struggle and the never-ending tension behind. I welcomed the comfort with open arms.

Deep down I wondered what the next trade-off might be. Would it come soon or would it build up over time, each day of happiness tainted with the fear of the opposite? After I'd spent a few days in my grandparents' backyard, watching my dad grill steaks and witnessing how he'd matured and learned to control his anger, he got a call from his doctor after a routine checkup.

"A few of your prostate antigen levels are high," the doctor said. "It'd be best if you come back for us to run some more tests." After an initial misdiagnosis, my dad received the news that he'd developed prostate cancer. By that time, it had progressed faster than anyone could have anticipated. Instead of planning trips to beach towns, I booked flights to Mexico City where he could see specialists.

"There's two types of prostate cancer," the doctor said. "One allows the host and parasite to coexist up until old age. Your dad has the other kind, the one that spreads and kills quickly." After the appointment, I overheard Dad talking to Mom on the phone, telling her about the road he had ahead. Although they had been separated for years, they were still a part of each other's lives. His voice cracked as he tried to hold back tears. The knot of sadness rose in my throat, but as I held back my own tears, they deteriorated into anger.

There was finally a sense of normalcy, of steadiness.
Why now? Why this? Why him?
Was it the corrosive dust in that goddamn factory?

How much is this going to cost?
Why am I their healthcare plan and their retirement plan?

Why are my other first-gen friends' parents able to sustain
themselves?
Why does everyone have to rely on me?

When will Fer get a job and finally help?
Why am I so selfish?

What if my dad dies while I'm over here bitching about the
anxiety I have because I have to provide for them?
Fuck.

In my mind's spiral, the image of the old white therapist I'd briefly seen came to mind. "It's important that you set boundaries," she'd said, as if setting boundaries with a Mexican family was an insignificant feat. I'd had no indication that I needed to return to the office for in-person work, so I canceled my return flight to New York. I planned to stay in Mexico indefinitely to make sure my dad received the best medical care possible.

———————

At the hospital, my dad was connected to an array of beeping machines, and the nurses permitted only one of us in with him at a time.

"This is basically the Ritz," I joked.

"I think this stay might be more expensive," he said, his smile bright. Like any respectable daughter, I made sure my dad would look fresh for his surgery. After setting up an iPad for him to watch movies while he waited, I coated his lips with a Laneige sleeping mask. Eventually the nurses let my mom come in, too. Together we FaceTimed Fer, who panic cried and laughed from his dorm room. When it was finally time for Dad to be taken in for surgery, the nurses picked him up as he looked toward us, embarrassed that they hadn't let him get in the wheelchair by himself. He looked small and cuddly as they rolled him away, his gown enfolding him in excess cloth. For the next few hours, we waited anxiously for updates as the surgery went on past the time they had estimated. As always, we stood in the in-between.

After what felt like an eternity, a nurse emerged to meet us. "The doctor is cleaning up and will be out in a second," she chirped.

On cue, the doctor emerged. "Surgery took longer than expected due to some old scars he had from a previous procedure," he explained as we waited for him to tell us what we really wanted to know.

"Is the tumor gone?" I asked impatiently.

"We'll have to wait for pathology to come back and confirm this, but it went as well as we could have hoped. You can breathe for now," he said with an encouraging smile. "Once he's awake, you can go in to see him."

Relieved, we went down the list of people waiting for a status update on my dad. Old friends, my grandparents, and of course, my little brother. Fer answered almost immediately, holding his breath as we told him the good news. In some ridiculous act of disassociation, Fer immediately shifted his focus to his spring break plans.

"I was going to buy my ticket back to New York for spring break," he began.

"Fer! I won't be back by then," I stammered, angry at my brother's personal priorities.

"Joke's on you," he replied. "I got my school to buy me a flight *home*," he screamed. After watching me turn trauma into gold, my brother had learned some tips and tricks.

"I told them that my dad had cancer and that my mental health is at an all-time low," he continued, making a joke out of shit situations like he always had. "Y pues ya sabes. I'll be there in a few days. Keep it a secret," he joked.

Not even a few days after surgery, my dad was out and about against doctor's orders, completely disregarding the catheter sticking out of his abdomen. Even after we collectively yelled at him, my dad shrugged us off.

"I want tacos de cabeza," he insisted. "I can drive myself there." Unable to stop him, I hopped into the passenger seat, wishing once again that I'd gotten my license at sixteen like everyone else. When we came back, with bags of tacos in hand, my mom and brother were waiting.

"Sorpresa!" Fer screamed, jazz hands and all. Comically, he went in for an awkward hug as he avoided Dad's healing wounds.

"I really thought I wouldn't see you again, mijo," Dad said. "I'm so happy that you're here."

After years apart, my family spent the rest of my brother's spring break together, laughing and getting on one another's nerves. Aunts and uncles came over for afternoon coffee and stayed well past sundown. Fer teased Dad about his new pee bag while simultaneously demanding that he follow directions.

"I'm not a dog. I do what I want," he jested while pointing to my dogs.

"Cálmate, Pa," I replied. "They're your grandkids."

"There you go again," my mom interjected as she picked Dasha up into her arms. "We want human babies in the family, too, don't we, Dasha," she cooed as Fer and I shot each other a look.

"The bloodline ends with us," we teased as Mom continued complaining to my cackling aunts.

"This generation is crazy," they concluded. By that point, the entire room was full of laughter. Before the world decided to spin and rebalance again, I savored the joy of having my family under one roof, wishing that I could capture the moment forever.

Before heading back to college in Vermont, my brother gave my dad a tearful goodbye, leaving snot on Dad's shoulder as he bent down to embrace him.

"Que alto estás!" Dad said as he patted Fer's back. "Don't worry, I'm going to be fine," he said, reading my brother's worry in the way that parents do. "I'll see you again before you know it." Fer, who hadn't been able to utter a word since the crying began, wailed harder.

"But that's, like, Christmas!" he gasped between sobs. In addition to my brother and dad, my grandma was also crying. The entire scene felt overdone.

"It's not like this is a funeral," I yelled over the noise as my mom shot me a death stare.

"It's okay for people to cry, Elizabeth," she reminded me. "Besides, you know how your brother is." Fer had always been good at expressing the feelings I held in. Eventually my mom and brother got into the car and we watched as they disappeared, making their way toward the border, to cross it on their way to the Phoenix airport. I stayed behind with my dad, trying not to dwell on the hole that Mom and Fer left. Though I knew that Mom would eventually swing back to check in, I knew that she wouldn't stay for long.

"You know I have my own place and that your dad has his," she reminded me when I asked her to stay. "Come visit me in a few weeks." I nodded, knowing full well that I wouldn't. Not while my dad was recovering. Instead, I logged on to my computer and tried to make strides at my new job, losing track of the days as my dad went to all his appointments. Even when the pathologists came back and confirmed the surgery's success, I remained somewhat paralyzed, expecting the tide to turn on us again.

Ultimately, it was my mom who shook me back into reality. "Estás loca, Elizabeth," she told me a few weeks later. "You need to get out of here. You can't get stuck in the town we worked so hard to get you out of." I shrugged my shoulders indifferently. With both hands on my shoulders, my mom faced me.

"Tu papá está bien," she said. "There is nothing for you to do here." I wanted to say, "Sure, he will be okay in the sense that his death isn't imminent, but not in the sense that there is universal healthcare and the systems that profit off disease and perpetuate poverty have been dismantled." But I refrained, choosing instead to believe her and booking a flight to the Oaxaca Coast a week later.

––––––––––

While I was drowning in one of my college classes, a professor told me something that had given me a little room to breathe. "The key to learning is finding a single bead of a lesson to take with you," he said. "As you go through life, that bead will turn into a rosary of knowledge, guiding you toward the right path." Although I wasn't religious, I'd put my faith in my education. No matter how much uncertainty there was in my life, it had remained a constant, shielding me from loneliness and uncertainty. As I looked out into the ocean off the Oaxaca Coast, I wondered if I would ever be able to let myself get swept up in the currents rather than fighting against them. I wondered if I'd ever be able to ride life's waves with stability and strength.

From a distance, a group of surfers stepped out of the water, their feet sinking in the hot sand as they sprinted toward me.

"The sand is hot," yelled my friend Bruno, as his girlfriend Jenna trailed behind him.

"You gonna get in?" Jenna asked me. "You can use my board. I'm done."

"I think it would be a waste of a trip if I didn't get in the water at least once," I replied, walking over to the foam surfboard she'd set down. I didn't get far before I was stopped in my tracks.

"Estás loca, you can't go out there." Carlos, a young Oaxacan surfer who'd come with our group, said, laughing. "Siéntate. I'll give you a free homie lesson on how not to die out there." Like a diligent student, I listened, hoping that one lesson would be enough.

Once we were in the water, Carlos pushed me toward an undertow. "It's like a freeway," he'd explained. "We use undertow currents to get us to the back line faster. You won't get as tired if you take the path."

Before I knew it, my friends on the coast became tiny dots. Unbound by the borders and restrictions of land, I paddled along toward the break point. I wanted a chance to try life without fear, without worrying about the guilt of feeling joy. As the wave gathered behind me, I listened for Carlos's cue.

"Stand!" he yelled. For a fraction of a second, I stood up, my heart racing with adrenaline as the wave pushed me closer to the shore. In shock, I looked down toward my feet, trying to make sure that they were positioned as I'd been taught. When I did, I lost my balance, tumbling into the water, where the sound of Carlos and my friends cheering me on faded. I held my breath as the waves pulled me down, rolling my body in ways out of my control. Carlos had warned me that this would happen, urging me to stay calm when it did. "You might not know up from down right away, but you'll find the surface."

For years, I had been fighting currents. Currents that tried to keep me away from the people that I loved; currents that tried to stop me from moving forward. While some of the currents kept me intensely focused on my education, others made me constantly wonder if I was a good daughter and if I was doing enough to protect and take care of my family. I remembered the Rillito, full of living things fighting to survive. After tumbling under the surface for a few seconds, I could finally see the sun beaming down, guiding me up toward the air. Out of the danger zone, I grabbed the board and paddled back toward the shore, my friends still screaming with excitement. As I got closer, I wondered if some of the same currents I'd been fighting were simply trying to guide me somewhere closer to where I needed to be—closer to who I really am. Because out in the water, I *am* an ordinary Brown girl, letting the waves crash over me, just learning how to surf.

ACKNOWLEDGMENTS

It's a miracle that we've even gotten to the acknowledgments section. This wouldn't have been possible without my family—my mom, dad, and brother. I hope I am making you proud. Mi tío Gabriel y tía Denia, who gave me a home when I most needed it. To my grandparents, whose endless knowledge and spirit I try to carry with me. To my friends who also asked me, "How's the book going?" I'm sorry for ghosting you when you asked. You better rate it five stars on Goodreads.

To the team who helped me get this book into a readable condition—thank you. Johanna Castillo, my incredible agent, I am starstruck by you. I still cannot believe you took a chance on my silly little self. To my editor, Hannah Phillips, thank you for being so patient, and I am so sorry for all the extensions and chaotic emails you have dealt with. I probably won't change but your support means everything. To Noelle Olmstead, who thoughtfully helped me craft the jumbled mess of thoughts and text I had into a coherent set of twenty-seven chapters. I'm so glad we finally have a book.

To the educators I've had along the way. The teachers of Flowing Wells School District, who were there when I needed adults to take care of me, who nurtured my curiosity and fed my large ego. The students under your care are lucky to have you; please never give up the fight. To the professors at Penn, who reminded me that I was worthwhile and had value even when I felt like I didn't, you saved me when I was most vulnerable. The little beads of knowledge you gave me are ones I will forever hold close.

Lastly, to my dogs, Yoshi and Dasha, who chaotically distracted me every time I had a mental breakdown. You are a good boi and a good girl.

NOTES

9. Holy Wars

On April 23, 2010: Alisa Reznick, "'Show Me Your Papers': A Decade After SB 1070," Arizona Public Media, July 30, 2020, https://news .azpm.org/p/news-splash/2020/7/30/177558-show-me-your-papers -a-decade-after-sb-1070/.

10. Fool's Gold

real threat to safety: "Number of Mass Shootings in the United States Between 1982 and April 2023, by Shooter's Race or Ethnicity," Statista, https://www.statista.com/statistics/476456/mass-shootings -in-the-us-by-shooter-s-race/.

16. Earth Camp

named after the white plaster: "Living Inside the Rock: The Cliff Dwellings of Canyon de Chelly," East West Quest, http://www.eastwestquest .com/canyon-de-chelly/#:~:text=The%20White%20House%20Ru- ins%2C%20so,guide%20or%20a%20park%20ranger.

The canyon became a National Monument: "Canyon de Chelly: History That Echoes Through the Canyons," National Park Reservations,

https://www.nationalparkreservations.com/article/canyondechelly
-rich-history/.

"The canyon is thought of": Cindy Yurth, "Woman Drowns in Flood-
Swollen Canyon," *Navajo Times*, August 3, 2015, https://navajotimes
.com/reznews/woman-drowns-in-flood-swollen-canyon/.

23. Betty Crocker's Recipe for Success

"one of the most sophisticated": "Huntsman Hall, Jon M.," Penn Facilities &
Real Estate Services, https://www.facilities.upenn.edu/maps/locations
/huntsman-hall-jon-m.

25. Working Sister

proven in other places: Wallace Ludel, "Fourth Suicide Shuts Down New
York's Towering Vessel Yet Again," *The Art Newspaper,* July 30, 2021,
https://www.theartnewspaper.com/2021/07/30/fourth-suicide
-shuts-down-new-yorks-towering-vessel-yet-again.